India and Southeast Asia

International Politics in Asia Series
Edited by Michael Leifer, London School of Economics

China and the Arms Trade
Ann Gilks and Gerald Segal

Soviet Foreign Policy in Southeast Asia
Leszek Buszynski

ASEAN and the Security of South-East Asia
Michael Leifer

China's Policy Towards Territorial Disputes: The Case of the South Sea Islands
Chi-kin Lo

INDIA AND SOUTHEAST ASIA

Indian Perceptions and Policies

MOHAMMED AYOOB

PUBLISHED UNDER THE AUSPICES OF THE
INSTITUTE OF SOUTHEAST ASIAN STUDIES,
SINGAPORE BY

ROUTLEDGE

London and New York

First published 1990
by Routledge
11 New Fetter Lane, London EC4P 4EE

Simultaneously published in the USA and Canada
by Routledge
a division of Routledge, Chapman and Hall, Inc.
29 West 35th Street, New York, NY 10001

© 1990 Mohammed Ayoob

Typeset by LaserScript Limited, Mitcham, Surrey
Printed and bound in Great Britain by Mackays of Chatham

British Library Cataloguing in Publication Data

Ayoob, Mohammed
  India and Southeast Asia : Indian perceptions and
  policies. – (International politics in Asia Series)
  1. India (Republic). Foreign relations
  I. Title II. Institute of Southeast Asian Studies
  III. Series
  327.54

ISBN 0-415-03894-4

Library of Congress Cataloging in Publication Data

Ayoob, Mohammed, 1942–
  India and Southeast Asia : Indian perceptions and policies /
  Mohammed Ayoob.
      p.   cm. —— (International politics in Asia series)
  Includes index.
  ISBN 0-415-03894-4
  1. Asia, Southeastern—Foreign relations—India. 2. India—
Foreign relations—Asia, Southeastern. 3. India—Foreign
relations—1947–1984. 4. India—Foreign relations—1984-
I. Institute of Southeast Asian Studies. II. Title. III. Series.
D525.9.U6A96   1990
327.54—dc20   89–10377
                                                  CIP

Contents

Preface

This study attempts to analyse first, how Indian policy-makers and groups influential in the foreign policy-making process perceive the importance of Southeast Asia within the overall Indian foreign policy framework; and, second, what sort of policies have emerged, or are likely to emerge, from these perceptions, and how far they have served, or are expected to serve, India's political and strategic objectives. In order to be meaningful, any analysis of such perceptions, and their subsequent translation into policies, has to be put in the context of the broad Indian foreign policy and strategic design as well as that of India's relations with, and approach towards, this region since Indian independence in 1947. The first two chapters, which comprise nearly a quarter of the total text, have attempted to provide precisely these contexts so that the reader can decipher both the changes and continuities in Indian perceptions of, and policies towards, Southeast Asia in the present decade.

Chapters three to seven are the major part of the book, and analyse current perceptions of the Indian foreign policy and defence community of Southeast Asia, its two main sub–regions, ASEAN and Indochina, and the major international issues affecting relationships both within and among these two sub–regions. These chapters also analyse Indian perceptions of the linkages between Indian interests in Southeast Asia and other major Indian foreign policy and security concerns, particularly in the larger Asia-Pacific region. These chapters further examine the connection between these perceptions and the policy followed by the Indian government towards the region as a whole, towards the major regional actors, and towards important regional issues that are of international significance. The eighth, and last chapter focuses on the common themes to emerge out of this study, and locates them within the broader context of Indian strategic and political interests.

This study is primarily focused on the strategic and political dimensions of Indian policy towards, and interactions with, Southeast Asia. This reflects the intellectual bias of the author on the one hand, and his firm conviction that economic considerations, although increasingly important in India's policy calculus towards this region, are clearly secondary in terms of their influence on the policy output as compared to political and strategic factors.

It is impossible to analyse perceptions scientifically except on the basis of questionnaires sent out to a random sample of the universe whose perceptions one is engaged in analysing. This is a method which obviously one cannot follow when attempting to analyse perceptions of a country's foreign policy and defence community, especially when one is interested in perceptions regarding such sensitive subjects as a country's strategic design and its foreign policy framework. A great deal, therefore, depends on the analyst's access to, and rapport with, both the policy-making community and the larger group of influential individuals who presumably have an input into the policy-making process, and, in the final analysis, to his intuitive judgement based on his familiarity with the subject and his ability to separate the grain from the chaff. I undertook the present study in the knowledge that, while my analysis of Indian perceptions might occasionally diverge from the reality of such perceptions, this risk was worth taking because of my confidence that I was in a better position than most others to undertake the project since I met most of the criteria for the successful completion of this task.

A substantial part of the analysis in chapters three to seven is based on my interviews and conversations in November–December 1986 and May–June 1987[1] with members of the Indian foreign policy and defence community, including active and retired politicians who have participated in the Indian foreign policy-making process in one capacity or another, serving and retired senior bureaucrats of the various ministries and departments involved in making foreign and defence policies as well as some serving and retired senior officers of the armed forces. These interviews have been supplemented by my conversations with defence and foreign policy analysts among academics and journalists, and with representatives of trade and industry. Published works reflecting the views of segments of the Indian foreign policy and strategic community have also furnished me with essential clues to the thinking of the Indian policy-makers and the larger foreign policy elite. General books and articles on Indian foreign and defence policies, which I have read and reread over many years, have, of course, provided me with much of the essential background for the project.

Given the nature of my primary sources, it is not possible for me to identify them or link them to every formulation I have made about Indian perceptions and policies. This is because most of the analyses and views that were communicated to me were given on the understanding that the source or sources would remain anonymous, both because of the sensitive nature of the subject and, often, of the positions occupied, either currently or previously, by my sources. The second reason why I have not identified my sources is that the perceptions that I have referred to are, in the case of the overwhelming majority, not those of one person. They have often been arrived at by grafting different peoples' views on each other in an architectonic fashion so as to construct a single and meaningful whole.

While I owe a debt of gratitude to many people in New Delhi, within and outside the government, who talked to me freely about the subject of my research and helped me in many other ways, I would particularly like to thank the Institute for Defence Studies and Analyses (IDSA), New Delhi, and its past and present directors, Mr K. Subrahmanyam and Air Commodore Jasjit Singh, for providing me with office space and research facilities during the time I spent in New Delhi in connection with this project. Had it not been for their kind assistance, it would have taken me much longer to complete this study. Dr G. V. C. Naidu, a young and talented researcher at IDSA, also deserves special thanks for helping me in various ways in connection with this project.

I am most grateful to Professor K. S. Sandhu, Director, Institute of Southeast Asian Studies, Singapore, for his advice, encouragement and, especially, for his perceptive comments on the first draft of this study. I am also grateful to the following friends for taking the trouble to read an earlier draft of the manuscript and for making extensive comments on it: Professor Stephen Cohen, University of Illinois, Urbana; Dr John Girling, Australian National University, Canberra; Mr Paul Kreisberg, Carnegie Endowment for International Peace, Washington, DC; and Dr Leo Rose, University of California, Berkeley. Their suggestions and constructive criticisms have contributed a great deal to the improvement of the quality of the final product. I would also like to thank the two anonymous reviewers of the manuscript for pertinent comments on, and suggestions regarding, the manuscript which helped to refine my arguments and sharpen my conclusions. Of course, I alone bear the responsibility for the interpretations and conclusions, as well as the shortcomings, of this study.

Singapore October 1988

Note

1 These have not been the only times when the issue of Indian foreign policy and strategic perceptions has come up in my conversations with members of the Indian foreign policy and strategic community. I have had a continuing dialogue with them for the last two decades, including many working visits to New Delhi during the past thirteen years that I have been living outside India.

1

India's Foreign Policy Framework and Strategic Perspective

Before one can begin to examine either Southeast Asia's importance to India in terms of its foreign policy objectives and its strategic interests or the importance that India has, or might come to have in the near future, for the security environment of Southeast Asia, one must have a clear picture of India's broad foreign policy framework and its overall strategic perspective. This is extremely important because, without the awareness of this larger canvas, it would be impossible to decipher the entire range of Indian interests· in Southeast Asia, to assign comparative weight to these various interests, and realistically to evaluate the type and amount of capabilities that India is likely to devote to the protection and furtherance of its interests in the region. In other words, without such a framework it would be impossible to locate the position and importance of Southeast Asia in the Indian scheme of things and to assess the kind of role that India is likely to play in the international politics of the Southeast Asian region for the rest of this century.

The basic framework of Indian foreign policy that can be distilled from its actions in world affairs during the forty years of its independence comprises the following major elements:

(a) A world-view shaped both by the movement for national independence and by the nationalist leaders' perception of India's past and their aspirations for its future;

(b) The coincidence of the emergence of a bipolar world following the Second World War, with India's emergence as an independent actor on the world scene;

(c) The threats to, and the problems for, India's security that emerged directly from the partition of the British Indian empire and, therefore, the disruption of India's strategic unity that had been accepted as a given fact during the period of the Raj;

(d) The emergence of China as a major Asian actor following the Communist victory of 1949, two years after India's independence, and China's annexation of Tibet the following year (1950) thus bringing Chinese presence and power in direct contact with India on the latter's northern and northeastern borders;

(e) The need for fruitful economic interaction with the rest of the world in terms of trade, aid, and investment, which was considered crucial for India's developmental goals.

The enmeshing of these fundamental concerns in various forms and at different times has, by and large, determined the broad contours of Indian foreign policy, including its policy towards Southeast Asia as a whole and towards the individual countries that comprise this region. It is, therefore, important for us to examine the major consequences for Indian foreign policy that have emerged out of the interplay of these variables over a period of time.

The Indian elite's world-view, shaped as it was by the anti-colonial movement and the deliberately generated nationalist 'myths' about the greatness of the country's past, became operational in two ways that were relevant to India's foreign policy. First, it generated an anti-colonial, therefore, anti-hegemonistic foreign policy ethos. It meant that Indian policy-makers refused to accept the legitimacy of the argument that the major powers in the international system had the right to determine the fundamental issues of world order exclusively on the basis of their military, industrial, and technological might. Second, it meant that the 'power-vacuum' theory which had become fashionable in the West in the aftermath of decolonization, particularly in relation to the then prevailing situation in Asia, was treated with scepticism if not derision by the Indian elite. This theory was perceived as an instrument for the reintroduction of Western presence into Asia through the backdoor and an intellectual apology for what had come to be known as 'neo-colonialism'. In a word, this world-view provided the mainspring for the Indian aspiration to act independently of the 'managers' of the international system and to judge every major international issue on its own merits and/or on the basis of its effects on India's vital national interests.

The post-war configuration of global power reinforced the Indian elite's proclivity for autonomous action in the international political sphere. The Indian reaction to the rigidity in the international system introduced by the strategic and political bipolarity of the immediate post-war years was best encapsulated in the term 'non-alignment',[1] a concept that became increasingly popular in many other decolonized polities as well. This was not a policy of mechanical equidistance from both the poles of global power but an attempt to maintain India's capacity to decide the basic thrust of its foreign policy without dictation by either superpower. The rejection of the rigidity of alliance systems conceived in the context of the Cold War was the logical corollary of this policy. A further corollary was the Indian attempt, largely unsuccessful, to keep Asia, and especially South Asia, free from Cold War competition and conflict. Although in the process of implementation this policy had to be modified periodically to take account of certain contingencies as they arose, the basic thrust of India's non-alignment has survived the ups and downs that the country, and, therefore, its foreign policy, have undergone in the four decades of its independent existence.

The disruption of India's strategic unity in 1947, the emergence of Pakistan as an independent state in the northwest and northeast of the subcontinent and the basically hostile relationship between the two successors to the British Indian empire, not merely created an unprecedented security problem for India (in the sense that it introduced a fundamental discontinuity in the Indian strategic environment), it also embroiled the subcontinent in global Cold War issues, thus defeating the Indian objective of keeping South Asia free from Cold War rivalry. Pakistan, obsessed by its need and desire to balance India's inherent power superiority in the subcontinent, aligned itself with the United States in the early 1950s and signed not only a Mutual Defence Assistance Pact with Washington but joined SEATO and the Baghdad Pact (later renamed CENTO) as well. The United States, having been unsuccessful in its attempt to woo India into its web of anti-Soviet alliances, was willing to accommodate Pakistani interests in its overall strategic scheme. Washington, thereby, succeeded in alienating India and paving the way for the growth of friendly and mutually profitable relations between New Delhi and Moscow.[2] The pattern of India–US–Soviet relationship established in those early days of the Cold War has by and large survived to this day.

This pattern has been reinforced by India's concern with China. The Communist takeover of China in 1949 led to the emergence of a unified and potential great power in Asia. The subsequent assertion of Beijing's authority over quasi-independent Tibet also meant that this potential great power was now India's next-door neighbour with a direct presence on India's Himalayan borders. If the process of partition destroyed India's British-imposed strategic unity, the Chinese annexation of Tibet removed the buffer between India and China which the British had successfully maintained between the two largest countries of Asia. The change of status quo in Tibet was beyond India's capacity to prevent given its limited trans-Himalayan capabilities, its preoccupation with the problems of the subcontinent following partition, and the dramatic increase in the military capability and the political will of the central government in China following the revolution. However, this change was to have immensely important implications for the future of Sino-Indian relations and of the Asian balance of power as a whole. As we will discuss later, the nature of the Sino-Indian equation has had important effects on India's policy towards Southeast Asia on the one hand, and on Southeast Asian perceptions of India on the other.[3]

The emergence of China as a major power centre in Asia also had substantial impact, both in positive and negative terms, on many other dimensions of Indian foreign policy. First, China's militantly anti-colonial and anti-capitalist stance coupled with its aspirations for autonomy of action similar to those of India strengthened India's bargaining power with the West. This resulted from the fact that in the context of China's revolutionary rhetoric the reformist demands that India made on the managerial powers of the international system appeared both moderate and reasonable. Furthermore, China's alignment with the Soviet Union, which lasted through the 1950s, added to India's importance in Western eyes both as an alternative model of economic development to China's in the newly independent countries of Asia and as a potential, if non-aligned, balancer of what was then perceived as the monolithic Sino-Soviet Communist bloc on the Eurasian landmass.

However, the negative implications of Chinese power in close proximity to India far outweighed the positive implications for

New Delhi. These included: (a) China's support, both political and military, for Pakistan in its disputes with India, once Sino-Indian relations began to deteriorate from the late 1950s onward; (b) Beijing's encouragement, particularly after the Tibetan uprising of 1959 and the Indian decision to give refuge to the Dalai Lama, of anti-Indian sentiments in the sub-Himalayan monarchies of Nepal, Bhutan, and Sikkim which were considered by India as falling within its strategic perimeter; (c) China's support in terms of military training and the supply of weapons to the various tribal insurgents in northeastern India, especially the Nagas and the Mizos; (d) the support extended by China, particularly in the 1960s and the early 1970s, to revolutionary Marxist (Maoist) movements, especially in West Bengal; (e) the complications introduced into Indo-Soviet relations in the late 1950s and early 1960s as a result of the deterioration in Sino-Indian relations; (f) the development of a two-front threat, one from China and the other from Pakistan, from the early 1960s onward, which led to a major escalation in India's defence expenditure, especially following the military debacle of the Sino-Indian border war of October–November 1962; and (g) the threat, in New Delhi's perception, of China, Pakistan, and the United States colluding against India's vital national interests following the Sino-American rapprochement beginning in 1971. The parallel US and Chinese policies on the Bangladesh crisis of that year and in relation to the subsequent war between India and Pakistan epitomized for India the sort of threat such a collusion could pose to what New Delhi considered to be its rightful role in the subcontinent.

The imperatives of economic development and, therefore, of profitable economic interaction with the rest of the world in terms of trade, aid, and investment, meant that relations with the Western industrialized countries of North America and Western Europe dominated the pattern of India's economic interaction during the first decade of the country's independent existence. This position of Western economic dominance began to erode from the late 1950s onward, as much for political as economic reasons, as India began to diversify its economic contacts by building mutually profitable relations with the Soviet Union and the socialist countries of Eastern Europe.

An additional aspect of this economic diversification was the Indian commitment to promote, what is now fashionably called,

South–South relations, i.e., to increase trade, joint ventures and technological collaboration with other developing countries. However, it was not until the 1970s that this aspect of India's foreign economic policy began to make a modest impact on the overall pattern of the country's economic relations. This was the result of a number of factors including the established patterns of India's trade with the West (partially modified by the growing interaction with the Socialist bloc), the lack of complimentarity among the economies of the developing world, as well as the established patterns of the other developing countries' economic interactions, which were, once again, heavily tilted in favour of the Western industrialized world. As we will discuss later, India's economic transactions with the countries of Southeast Asia, particularly those in ASEAN, have come to form an important component of India's South–South trade and investment policy.

Notes

1 For an attempt at a systematic analysis of the Indian policy of non-alignment and its linkages both with India's political culture and the international environment, see A. P. Rana, *The Imperatives of Nonalignment: a Conceptual Study of India's Foreign Policy Strategy in the Nehru Period*, Macmillan, Delhi, 1976.

2 For an overview of Indo-Soviet relations, see S. Nihal Singh, *The Yogi and the Bear*, Allied Publishers, New Delhi, 1986. For an in-depth study of the early period of Indo-Soviet relations, see Arthur Stein, *India and the Soviet Union: the Nehru Era*, Chicago University Press, Chicago, 1969.

3 For a perceptive discussion of Sino-Indian relations in the 1950s with special reference to South East Asia, see Ton That Thien, *India and Southeast Asia, 1947–1960*, Librairie Droz, Genève, 1963, 29–31 and 285–307.

2

Southeast Asia's Importance in Indian Foreign Policy: the Background

Southeast Asia has been important for Indian foreign policy for a number of reasons:[1]

First, the nationalist leadership, i.e., the first generation of India's post-independence leaders, had perceived the anti-colonial struggles in Southeast Asia as indivisible from their own fight for freedom from colonial subjugation. The Indonesian and Vietnamese freedom struggles, especially the former, had been followed with great sympathy by the politically-conscious Indian public during the last years of the British Raj. The Congress leadership, with Jawaharlal Nehru as its foremost articulator on international issues, was convinced that the future of India was indivisible from the future of Asia, and particularly of Southeast Asia. It was no coincidence, therefore, that even before the formal dawn of independence the interim Indian government organized an Asian Relations' Conference in March 1947, and independent India performed its first high-profile act in international affairs by convening the Conference on Indonesia attended by fifteen nations in January 1949.

The major purpose of the 1949 conference was to express solidarity with, and support for, the Indonesian nationalist leadership and to put pressure on the Dutch government and its supporters to accelerate the process of Indonesian independence. There was a general belief among the nationalist elite in New Delhi that India's goal of preserving its autonomy of action in world affairs could be achieved only in the context of decolonization in the rest of Asia and in cooperation with genuinely independent governments in the continent's larger and more important states. In India's perception, Sukarno's Indonesia fitted this description better than any other Asian political entity in the late 1940s and during much of the 1950s and this explains in great part the Indian attempt to coordinate closely its international moves with Indonesia, particularly on issues of decolonization and those related to the policy of non-alignment.

In this context it is interesting to note that while the Indian leadership was as convinced of Ho Chi Minh's nationalist credentials as it was of Sukarno's and Hatta's, its attitude towards the Vietnamese freedom struggle against the French can be certainly classified as lukewarm when compared to its enthusiastic support to the Indonesian nationalists. This difference can be explained only with reference to the Communist-dominated character of the Vietnamese national movement as compared to the largely bourgeois and petty-bourgeois character of its Indonesian counterpart. Given the Indian leadership's own aversion to indigenous Communists and the recognition on its part that a Communist-dominated Vietnam (in those days of Stalin's 'two-camp' thesis and of the American conception of a 'free' world pitted against a presumably 'enslaved' one) would automatically become a member of one of the Cold War blocs, the Indian lack of enthusiasm for the Vietminh can be easily understood. The Communist victory in China, which bordered Vietnam, added to Indian reservations regarding the Vietminh, who were viewed at that stage as the Chinese Communists' natural and logical allies in Southeast Asia.[2]

Second, the strategic importance of Southeast Asia to India was evident to India's prospective policy-makers and strategic thinkers even before the transfer of power from British to Indian hands. The events of the Second World War, especially the dramatic Japanese sweep through archipelagic and mainland Southeast Asia in a remarkably short time, had driven home the lesson to India's nationalist elite that India's eastern flank and the seaward approaches to the subcontinent were as important for India's defence as the land boundaries of the northwest and the north which had been the traditional concerns of strategists during the days of the British Raj. The latter attitude was understandable in the context of the British Indian empire because Britain was the unchallenged master of the seas around the subcontinent until the Japanese drive into Southeast Asia; however, it had to change under the dual impact of the Second World War and the withdrawal of British power from India.

The events of the war also increased Indian awareness of, and concern with, maritime strategy and the great importance of the Indian Ocean to the defence of the Indian peninsula. The lesson that India had lost its independence to European colonists because of the latter's control of the sea was relearnt by the Indian nationalist elite as a result of the experiences of the Second World War. In this sense, the strategic importance of Southeast Asia to India was enhanced in Indian perceptions, especially since it commanded the choke-points from which hostile naval forces could enter the Indian Ocean, particularly the Bay of Bengal. This point can be better understood in light of the fact that India's island territories in the Bay of Bengal lie barely 90 miles from the Straits of Malacca. Writing as early as 1945, one of the pioneers of strategic thinking in modern India, K. M. Panikkar, stated, 'The Gulf of Malacca is like the mouth of a crocodile, the Peninsula of Malaya being the upper and the jutting end of Sumatra being the lower jaw, *The entry to the Gulf can be controlled by the Nicobars and the narrow end is dominated by the island of Singapore.*'[3]

The third reason why Southeast Asia has been important for Indian foreign policy, is that the emergence of China as a major power in Asia bordering both India and Southeast Asia added another important dimension to Southeast Asia's strategic importance for India. From hindsight it becomes clear that, even during the heyday of Sino-Indian friendship in the mid-1950s, the Indians were both uneasy about the long-term prospects of the Sino-Indian relationship as well as aware of the importance of Southeast Asia, especially its non-Communist component, as a source of potential alliances against presumed Chinese expansionism. The Indian sense of unease was increased by the Chinese Premier's masterly performance in April 1955 at the First Afro-Asian Conference in Bandung, especially his conciliatory approach towards Western-aligned Pakistan. This Jawaharlal Nehru and his advisers considered an exercise in 'one-upmanship' at India's expense, particularly in the context of the fact that India had worked hard to overcome the apprehensions of several Asian countries regarding China's participation in that meeting.[4]

The Indian cultivation of both Indonesia and Malaya (later Malaysia) was important in this context. Unfortunately, from

India's point of view, when these two countries fell out with each other over the issue of the Malaysian Federation, its relations with Indonesia deteriorated, especially because Jakarta teamed up with Beijing in an attempt to destabilize the Southeast Asian situation. Malaysia reciprocated Indian support for the Federation by extending strong support to New Delhi on its border conflict with China. The Malaysian Prime Minister, Tunku Abdul Rahman, in fact, went to the extent of launching a fund in Malaysia in support of the Indian war effort.

It is also interesting to note in this context that India's attitude towards the anti-British insurgency following the Second World War and the reimposition of British control in Malaya was remarkably different from the one it adopted in regard to the anti-colonial insurgencies in Indonesia and Indochina. This difference can be directly traced to the nature of the Malayan insurgency which was Communist, largely confined to the ethnic Chinese in the country and with close links to the Chinese Communist Party. The combination of these factors made the insurgency in Malaya very suspect in the eyes of the Indian leadership even during the period 1948–57 when the British were in control of Malaya.[5] The continuation of the insurgency after the British withdrawal reinforced India's basically negative perception of the phenomenon.

These considerations regarding China also explain in large measure India's benign attitude towards the Five-Power Defence Arrangement among Malaysia, Singapore, Britain, Australia, and New Zealand, despite its opposition to security links between Asian countries and aligned Western powers in general, and the Southeast Asia Treaty Organization (SEATO) in particular. They also explain the cordial relations established by New Delhi with Saigon in the late 1950s and early 1960s as opposed to the cool but correct relationship with Hanoi during the same period, a relationship that was severely, although temporarily, damaged even further by North Vietnam's endorsement of the Chinese stand on the Sino-Indian border war of 1962.

The initial Indian response to the proposal for setting up a regional organization of non-Communist Southeast Asian states was also influenced by the twin Indian antipathies towards China on the one hand and the subversive aspects of Communism in Asia on the other. In fact, in the first half of 1967, the Indian government seemed to be positively interested in being invited to join such a grouping although it did not want to force its way into the projected organization. New Delhi's positive attitude towards ASEAN-in-the-making was demonstrated most clearly during the visit of the then Foreign Minister of India, M. C. Chagla, to Malaysia and Singapore in May 1967, when he strongly endorsed the idea of such a regional organization. In fact, he went further in his statement during his visit to Singapore and declared: 'We will be very happy to have bilateral arrangements with Singapore, with regard to trade, commerce, and economic cooperation. *But if Singapore chooses to join any regional cooperation, we will be happy to join such a grouping, if other members want India to do so.* If others want to have a small grouping, India will be very happy to remain outside and help such a grouping.... India does not want to dominate any regional grouping.'[6]

This Indian attitude was in sharp contrast to that of China, which strongly condemned the establishment of ASEAN. *Peking Review*, in its issue of 18 August 1967, published an article entitled 'Meeting in Bangkok: Puny Counter-revolutionary Alliance', in which it wrote: 'Bangkok was during August 5–8 a meeting place for the reactionaries of Indonesia, Thailand, the Philippines, Singapore, and Malaysia, that is, the handful of the United States imperialism's running dogs in Southeast Asia. There, with Washington pulling the wires, they conspired and formally knocked together a so-called "Association of Southeast Asian Nations" (ASEAN). This set up is an out-and-out counter-revolutionary alliance rigged up to oppose China, Communism, and the people, another instrument fashioned by the US imperialism and Soviet revisionism for pursuing neo-colonialist ends in Asia.... This reactionary association formed in the name of "economic cooperation" is a military alliance directed specifically against China.'[7]

However, after ASEAN was set up, the Indian attitude towards the organization, during the first few years of its existence, was somewhat ambivalent though never overtly hostile. This ambivalence was the result of two factors: one, India felt rather peeved at being left out of the grouping despite the strong signals it had sent expressing its interest in participating in the regional body; and, two, the presence of two members of SEATO – the Philippines and Thailand – in ASEAN. This second factor led to certain reservations among Indian policy-makers towards ASEAN since it detracted from

11

the non-aligned image of the organization and also because New Delhi felt that Pakistan could influence ASEAN in a way deleterious to Indian interests through its two SEATO allies within that organization.

It was not until 1973 that a joint communiqué issued by India with an ASEAN country mentioned the organization explicitly. The first such mention was made during the visit of the then Indonesian Foreign Minister, Adam Malik, to New Delhi in April 1973. The joint communiqué issued at the end of this visit noted that, 'The visiting Minister informed his Indian counterpart about the activities and the growth of the (sic) ASEAN, especially to safeguard the security, peace, and stability of the Southeast Asian region. It also noted that the Foreign Minister of India welcomed the progress achieved by the countries [of ASEAN] and the developments mentioned by the Indonesian Foreign Minister.'[8]

It is important to note that India's first official endorsement of ASEAN followed the Kuala Lumpur Declaration on ZOPFAN and the disbanding of SEATO. New Delhi apparently came to the conclusion that, with these two events, the foreign policy approaches of the ASEAN countries had shifted closer to India's traditional non-aligned stance on international affairs. However, it is worth mentioning here that even during the period 1967–73, New Delhi did not criticize ASEAN as an organization despite the divergence in the foreign policy orientations of the ASEAN countries on the one hand and India on the other, a divergence that became quite sharp following India's Friendship Treaty with the Soviet Union. The main reason for this restrained Indian attitude was New Delhi's calculation that given the anti-Communist predilections of all ASEAN members and the anti-Chinese predilections of a number of them, including not only Indonesia and Malaysia but also Thailand during that period, a working relationship with the organization was in India's long-term interests and could come in very handy especially if Chinese capabilities expanded in such a way in the future as to impinge on Southeast Asia in a major fashion.

The Indian policy of bolstering Burma politically and militarily immediately after the latter's independence can also be explained to a large extent with reference to Indian political and military concerns regarding the emerging power of Communist China in the common vicinity of both Burma and

India. The Indian support to Burma, which included military supplies, economic assistance and political endorsement of the U Nu government, was aimed both at preventing destabilization in its own volatile northeastern region (where tribal populations often straddled the India–Burma border), which could be taken advantage of by a strong China if it so desired, and at maintaining a friendly buffer between India and China.

These considerations were of paramount importance to New Delhi because it was fully cognizant of the fact that an unstable Burma, not in full control of its peripheral regions, could provide an ideal conduit for Chinese interference on India's tribal northeast, if, or rather when, Sino-Indian relations took an unfriendly turn. The fact that Burma was, and continues to be, plagued not only by ethnic but by Communist insurgencies as well, added greater weight to Indian concerns in this regard, particularly because Communist China was involved in supporting the Communist Party of Burma in the latter's efforts to destabilize the Burmese government by force.

Burma's strategic importance to India is also evident by the fact that the Japanese invasion of the northeast Indian territories of Nagaland and Manipur during the Second World War took place through Burma. Furthermore, the separation of East Bengal, now Bangladesh, from India in 1947 has added to the strategic isolation of the northeast from the rest of the country, especially from its centres of military power, and enhanced the logistical problems for New Delhi of meeting an external threat to these territories. This has, on the one hand, made the northeast more vulnerable to external intervention and, on the other, added to the significance of Burma as a strategic buffer between India and China. K. M. Panikkar had made the point as early as 1944 that, 'The defence of Burma is in fact the defence of India, and it is India's primary concern no less than Burma's to see that its frontiers remain inviolate. In fact no responsibility can be considered too heavy for India when it comes to the question of defending Burma.'[9] Indian relations with Burma were, however, frozen following the military coup of 1962 which ousted U Nu and initiated a policy of near-total isolation for Burma. Burma also withdrew from the Non-Aligned Movement (NAM) after the Sixth NAM Summit in Havana held in September 1979, accusing the movement of being 'non-aligned only in name due to the alignment of some members'.[10] However with Burma slowly emerging from this isolationist phase in the last few years, Indian contacts with that country, as symbolized by Prime Minister Rajiv Gandhi's visit to Burma early in 1988, have once again begun to increase.

Fourth, the presence of people of Indian origin in Southeast Asian countries, principally in Burma, Malaysia, and Singapore, also formed an input, although a relatively minor one compared to the political–strategic factors mentioned above, into Indian policy towards the region. The marginality of this factor was demonstrated dramatically when in the 1960s the military-dominated government in Burma launched a concerted policy aimed at the expropriation of Indian business and property, a policy which led to the exodus of large numbers of Indians from Burma to India during that decade.[11] In fact, the position of the sizeable, visible, and relatively prosperous Indian minority in Burma (a legacy of the fact that Burma was administered as a part of British India until the mid-1930s) had come under increasing attack from the early years of Burmese independence and a set of policies aimed at reducing their economic and political clout within the country had been followed by the Burmese government since that time.

However, despite the fact that these policies had begun to be implemented under U Nu, who was himself considered to be a great admirer of Nehru and a staunch believer in strong Indo-Burmese economic and security ties, the Indian government, to the considerable chagrin of certain special interest groups and some of its domestic opponents, did not allow the visibly deteriorating status of Indians in Burma and the discriminatory policies aimed at them to interfere with its policy of firm support to the Burmese government both in economic and security terms in order to help the country emerge as a viable nation-state.[12] This Indian support was tied to its broader objective of preserving a stable and united Burma on its eastern flank, an objective that has already been discussed above in the context of Indian strategy *vis-à-vis* China.

Although people of Indian origin in other parts of Southeast Asia did not suffer from the degree of overt discrimination that they did in Burma, the occasional problems that arose in this connection were always treated by the Indian government as minor irritants in India's relationship with the host countries rather than as major issues of national prestige. The overseas Indians in Southeast Asia soon came to realize their own minimal importance in the Indian foreign policy framework and, therefore, adapted themselves to the changing local situations more rapidly than would have been the case if active Indian support had been available to them in their struggle to preserve the privileges accumulated under colonial rule. As a result, the issue of overseas Indians did not affect India's relations with Southeast Asian governments in any major way and certainly could not be compared to the effect that the problem of the overseas Chinese had, and continues to have, on China's relations with some countries of Southeast Asia.[13]

Fifth, economic relations with Southeast Asia formed an important, although secondary, component of India's overall pattern of economic transactions with the outside world. A pattern of interdependence based on mutual needs of different primary commodities with which India and the various countries of Southeast Asia were endowed, coupled with easy access to each others' markets, formed the bedrock on which this superstructure of economic relations was constructed. Immediately after Indian independence, the Southeast Asian region, taken as a whole, ranked third, after the United Kingdom and the United States, in terms of India's foreign trade.[14]

However, from the early 1950s until the early 1970s, India's trade with Southeast Asian countries continued to decline in absolute and relative terms. This was the result, among other things, of the diversification of trading patterns on both sides, the 'green revolution' in India which made it self-sufficient in food thereby making the import of rice from Thailand and Burma redundant, and the different strategies of industrialization adopted by India on the one hand and the Southeast Asian countries on the other which led to changes in domestic demand both in India and in Southeast Asia. The decline of trade in relative terms between Southeast Asia and India until the early 1970s was dramatically demonstrated by the fact that India's share of Southeast Asian imports fell from 2.2 per cent in 1957–8 to a mere 0.5 per cent in 1972–3.[15] It was only in 1973–4 that this trend was reversed and from 1977–8 a marked growth in India–Southeast Asia trade was registered.[16]

Trade between India and the five countries of ASEAN during the 1970s increased dramatically. Between 1971–2 and 1979–80 the value of Indian exports to the ASEAN countries increased by 814.2 per cent, or at an annual compound rate of 28.0 per cent, much higher than the comparable growth rate of India's exports to the world as a whole, which grew at 16.7 per cent per annum. India's imports from ASEAN grew even more rapidly, registering an increase of 5,687.3 per cent between 1971–2 and 1979–80. This translated into an annual compound growth rate of 50.0 per cent, as compared to the annual compound growth rate of 19.2 per cent in India's imports from the world as a whole during the same period.[17] This growth was reflected in terms of ASEAN's share in India's total trade, which in 1971–2 stood at 1.5 per cent in terms of the value of exports and 0.39 per cent in terms of the value of imports. This share rose to a high of 4.2 per cent in the case of exports in 1978–9 (declining to 3.5 per cent in 1979–80) and a high of 5.2 per cent in the case of imports in 1978–9 (again declining in 1979–80 to 4.5 per cent). The 1970s also witnessed the reversal of the trade balance between India and the ASEAN member-states. India had a trade surplus with ASEAN as a whole until 1976–7, but from 1977–8 this turned into a deficit which has persisted until today.[18]

A relatively recent phenomenon, that of Indian investment in the form of joint ventures in the ASEAN countries, which began in the late 1960s, has also added considerably to the importance of Southeast Asia in the overall framework of India's international economic transactions. By the end of 1981 joint ventures in ASEAN countries approved by the Indian government constituted nearly 40 per cent of all such units approved internationally by New Delhi.[19] Therefore, by the end of the 1970s Southeast Asia had come to occupy a relatively important position in terms of India's foreign economic policy. It could be reasonably expected that this would have a spin-off effect on Southeast Asia's position in India's total foreign policy design.

The 1970s were, however, important for Indian–Southeast Asian relations in more than just the economic sphere. The year 1971, in fact, formed a major watershed in terms of India's perception of its role in international affairs, and particularly in the regions contiguous to the subcontinent. This perceptual change was directly related to India's victory over Pakistan in the war of December 1971, which led to the break up of Pakistan and the transformation of East Pakistan into the independent state of Bangladesh. The Indian political and military roles were crucial in bringing about this transformation. This event did not merely restore Indian military credibility, which had suffered immensely as a result of the debacle in the Sino-Indian border war of 1962, thereby forcing India into a period of political introspection; it also cut the Pakistani threat to India down to size, relegitimized India's preeminent position in the subcontinent and, consequently, released considerable Indian political and diplomatic energies, which had been tied up countering Pakistani manoeuvrings, for redeployment elsewhere.[20]

In the long run, this transformation of India's self-image was bound to have significant repercussions on Southeast Asian perceptions of India and on India's policy towards, and relationship with, the region. Unfortunately for India, in the short run, the importance of India's victory in the war of December 1971 was overshadowed by two other events which were perceived in Southeast Asia as having far greater significance in regional and global terms than the outcome of that war. The first of these was the Sino-American rapprochement, which coincided with the crisis over Bangladesh. This process became public with the dramatic visit to Beijing by President Nixon's National Security Adviser, Henry Kissinger, in July 1971 and reached its culmination with Nixon's trip to China in February 1972. It is interesting to note that Kissinger used Pakistan as the base for his secret flight to China, thereby emphasising the convergence of American and Chinese interests in regard to that country.

The second event which overshadowed the Indian victory in the Bangladesh war was directly related to the Sino-American rapprochement and the dramatic occurrence that heralded its approach. This was the Indian decision in August 1971, within a month of Kissinger's secret visit to Beijing, to sign a Treaty of Peace, Friendship, and Cooperation with the Soviet Union. The Indian decision was principally a response to the shift in the global balance of power that Kissinger's flight to Beijing portended and to the regional fall-out that it was expected to have, especially since it was perceived by India as a demonstration of the identity of Chinese and American interests and policies in regard to Pakistan and to the impending war between India and Pakistan over Bangladesh. From New Delhi's perspective, the treaty with the Soviet Union was aimed primarily, almost exclusively, at neutralizing any Chinese and/or American intervention on Pakistan's behalf which could frustrate the Indian strategy for the solution of the Bangladesh problem. The treaty, however, had unintended effects on India's image in the non-Communist countries of Southeast Asia, where it was perceived as seriously compromising India's policy of non-alignment. Moreover, since the ASEAN members' perceptions of the Soviet Union were far from benign, the Indo-Soviet Treaty tended to make them suspicious of Indian intentions as well.

Therefore, just when India's capabilities for greater involvement in Southeast Asia were about to be augmented, its credibility at least in non-Communist Southeast Asia was seriously eroded as a result of its treaty with the Soviet Union. Simultaneously, the transformation in the triangular relationship between the United States, the Soviet Union and China brought about by the Sino-American rapprochement led to the concentration of much of Southeast Asian attention on the likely future role of China in this region, to the almost total neglect of Indian potentialities for interaction with both Communist and non-Communist Southeast Asia.

There was a further reason why Indian relationships with Southeast Asia did not flourish as much as they should have in the 1970s, given the changes in India's regional security environment as well as the impressive increase in its technological and industrial capabilities. This was related to India's preoccupation throughout that decade with the region immediately to the west of the subcontinent, that is with the Gulf and the Middle East. As a result, Southeast Asia suffered from relative neglect on the part of New Delhi's policy-makers.

The dramatic increase in oil prices in the early 1970s, resulting from a tight energy situation, and the increasing assertiveness of the oil exporting countries, led to an unprecedented boom in the economies of the oil-rich countries, especially those in the Gulf with small populations and huge reserves. This combination of high oil prices and booming Gulf economies had important repercussions on India's policy towards these countries. Suddenly, the Gulf reached almost the top of New Delhi's foreign policy priorities and this led to a major concentration of Indian capabilities – economic, technological, and diplomatic – in that region. The importance of the Gulf in the Indian scheme of things can be explained by the fact that, on the one hand, India needed assured sources of oil supply at concessionary prices; and on the other, it was interested in carving out a share for itself in the booming oil-rich economies of the Gulf. Its large technologically skilled pool of manpower, its surplus capacity in terms of relatively cheap semi-skilled and unskilled labour and the considerable sophistication of its industrial and technological base provided India with the capability to export labour as well as technology (including turnkey plants) to the Gulf that were relevant to the needs of the oil-rich countries. This concentration of Indian energies in its western neighbourhood throughout the 1970s and into the early 1980s meant that New Delhi either could not pay adequate attention to its neighbours in Southeast Asia in diplomatic or economic terms, or did not feel that it was important to do so.

Notes

1 The Indian approach to Southeast Asia in the immediate post-independence years has been dealt with intelligently and quite comprehensively in Ton That Thien, *India and South East Asia, 1947–1960*, Librairie Droz, Genève, 1963, 55–80.

2 According to a leading specialist on India's relations with Indochina, 'Among the *real reasons* that restrained Nehru's enthusiasm for the Indochinese struggle were the character of the nationalist leadership in Vietnam and the continued French hold over five small possessions in India itself. After 1949, a third and more decisive factor was the emergence of a Communist regime in China, sharing a common border with a Communist-led movement in Vietnam. *The resulting attitude was one less of indifference or neglect than of calculated circumspection'.* D. R. Sardesai, *Indian Foreign Policy in Cambodia, Laos, and Vietnam, 1947–1964*, University of California Press, Berkeley and Los Angeles, 1968, 15 (italics added).

3 K. M. Panikkar, *India and the Indian Ocean: an Essay on the Influence of Sea Power on Indian History*, George Allen & Unwin, London, 1945, 21 (italics in extract added). A second edition of this book was published in 1961 and an Indian reprint was issued in 1971. This is the pioneering and probably the most significant study by an Indian strategic thinker on the importance of India's maritime environment for independent India's security. Panikkar came to the conclusion in this study that 'an exclusively land policy of defence for India will in future be nothing short of blindness. No other policy was required in the past, as the Indian Ocean was a protected sea – a British lake.... But today the position is different. The freedom of India will hardly be worth a day's purchase, if Indian interests in the Indian Ocean are not to be defended from India, especially, as in the changed circumstances ... the British fleet will be in no position to maintain that unchallenged supremacy which it possessed for 150 years.... As a free nation it is [India's] sacred duty to organise herself in every way for the defence of her freedom. This ... is primarily an Oceanic problem. Unless India

is prepared to stand forth and shoulder the responsibility of peace and security in the Indian Ocean, her freedom will mean but little. She will be at the mercy of any power which has the command of the sea, as it will be impossible for us to require of Britain or any other country to defend the Indian Ocean for us', 90–1.

4 However, according to George M. Kahin, who attended the Bandung conference as a reporter, one of the major objectives of the sponsors of the conference, particularly India and Burma, was the 'containment of Chinese and Vietminh military power and political influence at the southern border of China and the eastern boundaries of Cambodia and Laos, and the combatting of illegal and subversive Communist activities in all non-Communist Asia, particularly in their own countries'. George M. Kahin, *The Asian–African Conference*, Cornell University Press, Ithaca, 1956, 5.

5 According to one source, 'On his return from a Southeast Asian tour [in May 1949], B. V. Keskar, [Indian] Deputy Minister of External Affairs, said that the Malayan movement could not be described as a nationalist struggle, and that the insurgents there were nothing but bandits who do not care what or whom they opposed.' D. R. Sardesai, op. cit., 17.

6 Quoted in K. P. Saksena, *Cooperation in Development: Problems and Prospects for India and ASEAN*, Sage Publications, New Delhi, 1986, 53 (italics in extract added).

7 Quoted in G. V. C. Naidu, 'China and ASEAN', *Strategic Analysis*, vol.10, no.7, October 1986, 795. It must be noted, however, that the Chinese started to change their tune towards ASEAN in the early 1970s even before the Communist victories in Indochina. The change in Chinese policy was a function primarily of Sino-American rapprochement and deteriorating Sino-Vietnamese relations. This volte-face in China's attitude towards ASEAN resulted in the establishment of diplomatic relations with Malaysia, Thailand and the Philippines. According to Naidu, 'China's strongest endorsement of political and economic objectives of ASEAN came during Lee Kuan Yew's visit in May 1976 to China.' For details of Sino-ASEAN relations from 1976 onward, see pp. 796–804 of his article mentioned in this note.

8 K. P. Saksena, op. cit., 59–60.

9 K. M. Panikkar, *The Future of South East Asia*, Macmillan, New York, 1944, 46. Quoted in Ton That Thien, op. cit., 69.

10 Burma Socialist Programme Party, Central Committee Headquarters, *The Fourth Party Congress 1981: Party Chairman's Speech and Political Report of the Central Committee*, 1985, 43.

11 With the enactment of Burma's new Citizenship Law in 1982, the problem of the undefined status of people of Indian origin in that country has been solved to a large extent. However, the issue of compensation to Indians who left Burma during the mass exodus of 1963–7 has yet to be resolved. See R. G. Sawhney, 'Burma', in U. S. Bajpai (ed.), *India and its Neighbourhood*, Lancer International, New Delhi, 1986, 352.

12 According to a leading specialist on India–Burma relations, the Indian decision to treat the special interests of certain Indian groups in Burma, like the Chettiars (a south Indian business community which played an important role in the Burmese economy), as secondary to the primary Indian objective of bolstering Burmese national viability was taken in early 1949 'when the independent government of Burma seemed about to crumble under its multiple insurrections. New Delhi's reaction to Burma's 1947 Immigration Act and the 1948 Land Nationalization Act indicated a sympathetic attitude toward Indian special interests in regard to Burma. However, dating from Premier Nehru's February 1949 comment before parliament that 'petty difficulties' involving Indians in Burma should not be enlarged upon, a clearly sympathetic attitude by New Delhi towards Burma emerges.... Burma's insurrections had the side effect of placing the issues centering on Indian special interests in abeyance. These special interests never recovered their lost ground and their interest group activity tapers off markedly after 1950.' Richard J. Kozicki, *India and Burma, 1937–1957: a Study in International Relations*, unpublished Ph.D. dissertation, University of Pennsylvania, 1959, 452.

13 With the exception of those in Burma, overseas Indians in Southeast Asia did not possess even remotely the degree of economic power that the overseas Chinese had, or continue to have, in the various countries of the region and, therefore, did not arouse the hostility and suspicion of the indigenous population on the scale that the overseas Chinese have done. For a recent article on the overseas Chinese in Southeast Asia, see Keith B. Richburg, 'Asia's Overseas Chinese: Often a Distrusted Elite', *International Herald Tribune*, 21 March 1988.

14 Ton That Thien, op. cit., 74, Table VI.

15 Asis Kumar Majumdar, *South-east Asia in Indian Foreign Policy: a Study of India's Relations with South-east Asian Countries from 1962–82*, Naya Prokash, Calcutta, 1982, 215.

16 ibid., 216–19.

17 Charan D. Wadhva, 'India–ASEAN Economic Relations', in Charan D. Wadhva and Mukul G. Asher (eds), *ASEAN–South Asia Economic Relations*, Institute of Southeast Asian Studies, Singapore, 1985, 270.

18 ibid., 273.

19 ibid., 308.

20 For an analysis of the change in the power-balance in the Indian subcontinent as a result of the India–Pakistan war of 1971 and the emergence of Bangladesh, see Mohammed Ayoob, *India, Pakistan, and Bangladesh: Search for New Relationship*, Indian Council of World Affairs, New Delhi, 1975.

3

Southeast Asia in Indian Foreign Policy: Moving into the 1980s[1]

If the 1970s had seen the augmentation of Indian capabilities, economic, diplomatic, and military, that could have an influence on its capacity to act internationally, especially in areas of close proximity to the subcontinent, the first half of the 1980s seemed to provide the opportunity for India to redirect some of these energies away from its western neighbourhood to the region immediately to its east — Southeast Asia. At the same time the countries of Southeast Asia became more receptive to Indian diplomatic and economic overtures in the 1980s than they had been during the previous decade. Many factors contributed to this change in the mutual appreciation of each other by India on the one hand and the Southeast Asian states on the other.

Southeast Asian receptivity to Indian overtures increased as a result of two major shifts in Southeast Asian perceptions, one of which was related to China and the other to India's relationship with the Soviet Union.

First, the regional elites' preoccupation with working out the consequences for them of the dramatic Sino-American rapprochement of the early 1970s gave way to a more normal concern with the giant to their north. This, in turn, was the result of two interrelated factors. The first was that, by the beginning of the 1980s, the implications of the Sino-American rapprochement had been fully digested by the policy-makers of Southeast Asian countries, so much so that it had become an accepted part of the strategic and political landscape of the Asia–Pacific region. The second factor is that, at the same time, the limitations on Chinese capabilities to influence the Southeast Asian security environment, for good or ill, was also

22

fully understood and recognized by the regional leaders. These limitations were driven home especially by the less–than–creditable performance of the Chinese military in its invasion of Vietnam in 1979 following the latter's occupation of Kampuchea,[2] and the continuing uncertainties surrounding the economic and political future of China as it tried to zig-zag its way to modernity under the post-Mao leadership, which often seemed to be divided against itself.

Second, although the ASEAN governments continued to demonstrate a certain degree of unease regarding the Indo-Soviet Treaty, and while this unease seemed to increase, at least ostensibly, with the Indian soft-pedalling of the Soviet military intervention in Afghanistan and New Delhi's decision in July 1981 to recognize the Heng Samrin regime in Kampuchea, it was generally understood in the ASEAN capitals that India was not interested in acting as a surrogate for the Soviet Union in Southeast Asia or elsewhere. It was an open secret that despite India's refusal to condemn publicly the Soviet Union for its invasion of Afghanistan, New Delhi had privately conveyed its disapproval of the Soviet measure in no uncertain terms to Moscow. It was significant that Afghanistan was not mentioned in the joint communiqué issued by Leonid Brezhnev and Indira Gandhi at the end of the former's visit to India in December 1980, primarily because there was no common ground between the two leaders on the issue of the continued deployment of Soviet troops in Afghanistan to shore up the Marxist regime, itself weakened by internal divisions.[3] Again, despite their public rhetoric, ASEAN leaders were aware of the fact that India's stand on Kampuchea had more to do with New Delhi's equation with Hanoi and with the triangular relationship among India, China, and Vietnam, than with India's treaty obligations to the Soviet Union.[4]

On its part, Indian interest in Southeast Asia began to undergo a qualitative transformation, both for economic and strategic-political reasons, during the first half of the 1980s. The glut in the international oil market, the bickering within OPEC over pricing policy and production quotas, and the continued depression in oil prices despite the uncertainties connected with the Iran–Iraq war, sent clear signals to New Delhi that the end of the oil bonanza and, therefore, of the economic boom in the Gulf was near. This carried major implications for India's foreign economic policy since it reduced appreciably the attractiveness of the Gulf and the Middle East as markets for India's surplus manpower and for the country's technical and industrial expertise.

Furthermore, the continuing conflict between Iran and Iraq, two of India's most important economic partners in the Gulf, both in terms of oil supply and as markets for Indian technology, expertise, and manufactured products, led to an enormous drain on the resources of both countries and drastically reduced their capacity for mutually profitable economic transactions with India. Therefore, the Gulf war, the dramatic decrease in oil prices in 1986 (with the price of benchmark crude dipping below US $10 a barrel at one stage) and the fact that by the mid-1980s India produced two-thirds of its own oil requirements (compared to one-third at the turn of the decade) combined to downgrade further the importance of the oil-rich Gulf countries in India's foreign policy priorities.

Economic imperatives have, therefore, forced New Delhi to look elsewhere for alternative markets both for its surplus manpower and its technical and industrial expertise. From the perspective of India's policy planners, Southeast Asia, particularly ASEAN, appears to be a major logical alternative for the future redeployment of India's technological and economic capabilities following the further winding down of the Gulf economies. Since much of these capabilities will be relevant primarily to developing economies, they can be redeployed only in other developing regions. In Indian perceptions, the prospects for such redeployment are far superior in Southeast Asia compared to either Africa or Latin America, the first because of its relative poverty and the second because of its tremendous geographic and cultural distance from India.

The upsurge in India's economic interest in Southeast Asia has been complemented and, indeed, surpassed by an increase in the 1980s in New Delhi's strategic–political interest in the region. This, again, has been the result of multiple reasons, some of them related to India's growing disillusionment with the situation to the west of the subcontinent. The relative downgrading of the Middle East and the Gulf in India's foreign policy priorities has not been the outcome exclusively of economic factors. There seems to be a general feeling in New Delhi that India's preoccupation with its western neighbours has been politically counterproductive or, at best, futile. A feeling is abroad that the concentration of India's diplomatic–

political energies on West Asia has not brought commensurate results in terms of the attainment of India's major foreign policy objectives.

This assessment is partially the result of disenchantment with the seemingly unending conflicts in the Middle East and the Gulf, including the Arab–Israeli dispute, the Iran–Iraq war, and the conflict in Afghanistan with the last of these also possessing a 'proxy war' dimension as far as the two superpowers are concerned. These protracted conflicts have also had the effects of drawing the two superpowers into the region overtly and in increasingly direct confrontation with each other, a situation that New Delhi sees as threatening the stability of the international system as a whole. Moreover, such direct superpower involvement has curtailed India's capacity for diplomatic manoeuvring in West Asia, especially since New Delhi does not want unduly to offend either superpower regarding the highly emotive and contentious issues plaguing the region.

A further reason for India's downgrading of the West Asian region is related to the changing Indian perception of the 'Pakistan factor' within its overall foreign policy framework. This factor, especially the Indian desire to checkmate Pakistani activities in the predominantly Muslim Middle East, considered to be deleterious to Indian interests, had determined many of New Delhi's diplomatic postures in that region. Such a policy made a great deal of sense immediately after partition and independence, when Pakistan tried to emphasize its Muslim credentials in order to gain the sympathies of the Middle Eastern countries in its competition with India for power and influence in Asia in general, and in South Asia in particular.

It had, however, become very clear by the 1970s that the diplomatic postures and political alignments of the West Asian countries were based primarily on their assessment of their regime and state interests and their strategic relationship with one or the other superpower. While Pakistan could at times gain some marginal advantage over India on relatively unimportant issues by playing its 'Islamic card', these instances were so few and far between that they did not require the expenditure of Indian diplomatic and political energies far disproportionate to the actual threat they posed to Indian interests. This realization has gradually led to the diminution both of the 'Pakistan factor' in Indian foreign policy calculations towards the Middle East and of the inflated importance of the Middle East in Indian policy priorities which had been generated by the workings of this factor. One can reasonably expect that such diplomatic and political energies 'saved' from the Middle East would be used elsewhere with greater effect. Southeast Asia appears to be one of the prime contenders for the investment of these energies, given the current climate of opinion in policy-making circles in New Delhi.

Notes

1 A substantial portion of the analysis of Indian perceptions and policies beginning with this chapter and extending to chapter seven is based on my discussions in November–December 1986 and May–June 1987 in New Delhi with members of the Indian foreign policy and security community, which includes politicians, senior bureaucrats (both serving and retired), academics, and journalists involved in the analysis of India's foreign and defence policies. My sample, comprising both present and former decision-makers as well as professional analysts of Indian foreign and defence policies, has, I believe, provided me with a representative cross-section of expertise and opinion on the subject. My conclusions have, of course, been buttressed by my reading and rereading over the years of a large amount of published material on the subject and by frequent working visits to New Delhi.

2 According to Nayan Chanda, 'By crippling Vietnam's weak economy even further and by saddling it with the costly responsibility of defending the northern border against future Chinese attack, Peking ... raised the price that Hanoi would have to pay for opposing Chinese interests. But for all the sacrificing of soldiers and civilians – twenty thousand casualties by China's own estimate – and squandering of resources, the invasion achieved very little else.... Vietnam clearly had learnt no lesson, nor did the operation have any effect on Cambodia.... The most important lesson from the operation was perhaps learned by the Chinese themselves. A confidential Chinese report concluded that the Chinese and Vietnamese losses had been "about equal" and that the PLA had "not been able to conduct a modern war". Heavy casualties suffered during the war, as well as failures of weapons and tactics, brought home to China the urgent need for modernizing its military.' Nayan Chanda, *Brother Enemy: the War After the War*, Harcourt Brace Jovanovich, San Diego, 1986, 360–1.

3 The joint statement issued at the end of Gorbachev's visit to India in December 1986 also failed to contain any specific reference to Afghanistan, thus confirming the wide divergence in the Indian and Soviet positions on this issue.

4 For a recent analysis of this triangular relationship, see John W. Garver, 'Chinese–Indian Rivalry in Indochina'. *Asian Survey*, vol.27, no.11, November 1987, 1205–19.

4

India, China, and Southeast Asia

The relative downgrading of the 'Pakistan factor' following the 1971 war[1] and the reassessment made in New Delhi about Pakistan's long-term threat to Indian interests has also had another effect through a different route on Indian perceptions of the relative importance of Southeast Asia as compared to other regions, especially West Asia. This route has run through Beijing and the greater Indian concern with China following, first, the Sino-American rapprochement and, more importantly, China's entry into the post-Cultural Revolution phase and its launching of the 'four modernizations' programme. The projected increase in Chinese capabilities, both military and non-military, as a result of the modernizations programme and the transfer of sophisticated technology from the West, has caused great concern in New Delhi.[2] This concern has been heightened by the unresolved border problem between India and China,[3] and the fundamental wariness about Chinese intentions among India's policy-makers. The past history of Chinese military aid to Pakistan and recurring reports of Chinese collaboration with Pakistan on the latter's nuclear programme have augmented Indian apprehensions regarding China's capacity for 'mischief' in India's vicinity once Beijing has acquired the wherewithal to project power into South and Southeast Asia.

New Delhi's renewed preoccupation with China has, in turn, boosted the importance of Southeast Asia in the eyes of the Indian decision-making elite because of the region's close proximity to both India and China and the fact that it has been long considered a meeting ground of Chinese and Indian cultural and political influences. Just as the Indian obsession

27

with the 'Pakistan factor' had enhanced the importance of West Asia in New Delhi's calculations in the 1950s and the 1960s, the increasing Indian concern with the 'China factor' in the late 1970s and in the 1980s has worked to enhance the strategic and political importance of Southeast Asia in New Delhi's perceptions.

It is worth pointing out here, that even during the heyday of the Indian obsession with Pakistan, the more perceptive members of India's foreign policy and defence community were firmly of the opinion that, while Pakistan posed an immediate, short-term threat to Indian security, the long-term threat to India's security and its status in the international pecking order came from China. This view was, and is, based on the assumption that while conflict with Pakistan is a more likely possibility than a war with China in the short run, Pakistan's capacity, even with the help of sophisticated American weapons, to hurt India's vital interests is limited by the sheer asymmetry in indigenous resources that can be mobilized by the two neighbours in times of conflict. Furthermore, American support to Pakistan can be matched and neutralized by Soviet support to India, thereby making the outcome of an India–Pakistan conflict primarily dependent on the inherent resources and capabilities possessed by the two sides.

This, of course, gives India tremendous advantage except in the case of a two-front war, when New Delhi could be faced with coordinated attacks by both Pakistan and China. The acquisition of nuclear weapons by Pakistan is not expected to make a great deal of difference to this situation given the lead that India possesses over Pakistan in terms of nuclear technology. Even as strong an advocate of a nuclear India as K. Subrahmanyam has stated categorically that, 'We need not be unduly perturbed about Pakistan's nuclear capability. Once India decides to build an arsenal (though enveloped in ambiguity for the present) it is possible to establish a clear supremacy *vis-à-vis* Pakistan. With nuclear arsenals on both sides of the border there should be stability of deterrence. The Pakistani view, that with deterrence established the Kashmir issue can be reopened, does not make sense. On the other hand, such deterrence will stabilize the line of control in Kashmir into a border.'[4]

A recent report by a team of eighteen American specialists in nuclear arms and South Asian affairs, sponsored by the

Washington-based Carnegie Endowment for International Peace, has corroborated this assessment regarding India's potential superiority in terms of nuclear weapons *vis-à-vis* Pakistan. This report stated that it was possible that neither country had so far made complete nuclear bombs. It added, however, that by 1991 Pakistan could have as many as 15 Hiroshima-size bombs and that India could have more than 100.[5] To sum up, a Pakistani 'bomb' will merely give greater legitimacy to an Indian decision, when it is made, to manufacture and deploy nuclear weapons of greater sophistication and in larger numbers than those Pakistan is likely to produce. Coupled with the greater Indian sophistication in terms of delivery systems, as demonstrated by its successful testing in February 1988 of a surface-to-surface missile developed by Indian scientists and of an indigenously produced IRBM system with a range of 1,500–2,500 kms in May 1989,[6] it is clear that in the long haul Pakistan is in a 'no-win' situation as far as a nuclear arms race in the subcontinent is concerned.

In the light of this power asymmetry between India and Pakistan, it is understandable why the Indian perception of the 'Chinese threat' is almost exactly the opposite of such long-term complacency, but short-term preoccupation, with the threat from Pakistan. This conclusion is based on the calculation that not only has China in the past demonstrated its military superiority over India in the border conflict of 1962, but it is more than a match for India in demographic terms, and has built an impressive industrial and technological infrastructure which is reflected not only in its conventional military power but also in its capacity to produce and deliver sophisticated nuclear weapons.[7] It is in this context that Air Commodore Jasjit Singh, currently the director of India's leading think tank on strategic affairs, has argued in a recent article that: 'The appropriate and logical point of reference to define India's strategies would be in relation to the People's Republic of China. This is not only because China is placed in a geostrategic situation to provide the greatest challenges to the development of India as a global, Asian, and regional power, but also because China itself has set for itself a framework of reference in relation to the superpowers (and in the time perspective, year 2000) in the endeavour to enhance its power....A conceptual framework... [which emphasises] India's security in relation to China would not only take cognizance of the role and strategies of the superpowers (which are increasingly getting involved in activities uncomfortably close to India), but also provide a stabilizing influence in the international world order by moving towards an equitable power balance and help to provide stability in the Asian region.'[8]

One should note in this connection that India's efforts at attaining nuclear-weapons capability, demonstrated by the nuclear explosion of 1974, a decade after China's first nuclear test, were, and are, related more to the imbalance in the Sino-Indian nuclear equation than either to the Pakistan factor (which in fact acts as a brake on India's nuclear ambitions) or to the discriminatory clauses in the Nuclear Non-Proliferation Treaty (although these did form an important input into the Indian decision not to sign the treaty). The current ambivalent, if not totally negative, Indian stance on a Nuclear Weapons-Free Zone in South Asia, a proposal strongly advocated by Pakistan in the United Nations, is principally determined by the consideration that it would allow China to remain a nuclear weapons power while denying the same option to India. This is an extremely important consideration from New Delhi's perspective, because, as one Indian analyst has pointed out, 'While India would have a definite edge over China in a conventional war, in nuclear capability China is ahead of India by at least 15–20 years.'[9]

This assessment is borne out by K. Subrahmanyam, a leading Indian strategic thinker and former director of the Institute of Defence Studies and Analyses in New Delhi, who states: 'In the longer run it is China which will count more [than Pakistan] in Indian security calculations. At present China has a lead over India in missilery, nuclear weapon technology, nuclear propulsion and electronics, including computers. In terms of conventional equipment, however, India is relatively more favourably placed.'[10] In the same article Subrahmanyam has gone on to argue that, 'Any border agreement a nuclear India arrives at with a nuclear China will not look like an unequal agreement. Once the nuclear asymmetry is rectified, the two countries can afford to negotiate and work out a border settlement in a relaxed manner.'[11]

Moreover, many Indian strategic analysts clearly see a direct and positive relationship between China's demonstration of its nuclear weapons capability and the dramatic rise in its international status as well as its acceptance as a member of the club of great powers by the two superpowers and their other great power allies. This Indian perception has been best articulated in an article on Indian attitudes towards the Nuclear Non-Proliferation Treaty (NPT), written on the eve of the first NPT Review Conference in March 1975 by K. Subrahmanyam, who made the following observation: 'In 1954, the US Assistant Secretary of State, Walter Robertson, declared that it was the policy of the US government to adopt such a posture in Asia as to break up the Communist regime in China. Richard Nixon was the Vice President of that administration. The United States threatened China with nuclear weapons in 1953 and 1958, and Quemoy and Matsu were declared vital to US interests. But in 1972 Taiwan was quietly abandoned and President Nixon became solicitous about China's "legitimate interests" in South Asia. *Herbert Klein, the presidential aide, pointed out that 800 million Chinese armed with nuclear weapons could not be ignored. That is quite correct; 800 million Chinese could be ignored, as they were all these years, but not after 15 nuclear blasts at Lopnor and two earth satellites.*' [12]

It is in this context of India's self-perceived strategic inferiority *vis-à-vis* China that the latter's current modernizations programme, especially its upgrading of military equipment with the help of technology transfers from the West and Japan, its role as the balancer in the triangular balance of power in the Asia–Pacific region among the United States, the Soviet Union, and China, and recent moves towards rapprochement between Moscow and Beijing, have combined to heighten India's sense of insecurity in relation to its larger Asian neighbour. [13]

The last factor, the brighter prospects for a Sino-Soviet rapprochement, has particularly added to Indian concerns about the future direction of Chinese foreign policy, especially as it might pertain to China's immediate regional environment, which includes both Southeast Asia and the Indian subcontinent. The major Indian worry in this regard is related not so much to the effects of a thaw in Sino-Soviet relations on the Soviet-Indian relationship, as to its effects on Chinese policy in China's immediate neighbourhood once Beijing is relieved of the uncertainty, both political and military, which has for the past twenty-five years accompanied Soviet pressures on China's northern borders. The increasing aggressiveness in China's regional posture demonstrated in the confrontation with

Vietnam over the control of the Spratley islands in the South China Sea in March 1988 is bound to increase such Indian concerns since it is generally perceived as being linked to the thaw in Sino-Soviet relations and the consequent Chinese assessment that Moscow's reaction to Chinese moves against Vietnam, short of an all-out conflict, will be relatively mild and non-threatening as far as Beijing is concerned.

These Indian concerns have led to an increase in India's interest in Southeast Asia, with the objective of finding complementarity of interests with countries of the region in an attempt, among other things, to contain the likely growth of Chinese influence and reach in Southeast Asia. In New Delhi's perception, an increase in Chinese influence in Southeast Asia could possibly embolden Beijing also to challenge India on the latter's doorsteps in South Asia, particularly in the sub-Himalayan kingdoms of Nepal and Bhutan, or alternatively, to gang up with Pakistan to teach India yet another 'lesson'. China's policy of alternately blowing hot and cold in the last few years at the on-again off-again border negotiations between the two countries, and the escalation of China's hostile rhetoric regarding territories in northeastern India considered 'disputed' by Beijing, have been viewed by New Delhi as part of a Chinese strategy that does not rule out renewed confrontation with India.

Notes

1 This factor has once again achieved greater salience in terms of public debate, if not official thinking, in India following Pakistan's single-minded but dual-track (reprocessed plutonium and enriched uranium) strategy for the attainment of nuclear weapons capability. For a balanced account of Pakistan's search for nuclear weapons capability and the problems it has created. or is likely to create, for Pakistan and its neighbours, see Rasul B. Rais, 'Pakistan's Nuclear Program: Prospects for Proliferation', *Asian Survey*, vol.25, no.4, April 1985, 458–72. Indian allegations of Pakistani support to Sikh terrorism in the Indian state of Punjab has also increased, in public perceptions, the 'Pakistani threat' to India.

2 For a recent analysis of the likely impact of China's modernizations on regional security and the global balance of power, see Robert G. Sutter, 'Implications of China's Modernization for East and Southeast Asian Security: the Year 2000', in David M. Lampton and Caterine H. Keyser, *China's Global Presence: Economics, Politics and*

Security, American Enterprise Institute for Public Policy Research, Washington DC, 1988, 203–18.

3 For an account of recent attempts at normalizing Sino-Indian relations, see Nancy Jetly, 'Sino-Indian Relations: a Quest for Normalization' *India Quarterly*, vol.42, no.1, January–March 1986, 53–68.

4 K. Subrahmanyam, 'India's Security Challenges and Responses: Evolving a Security Doctrine', *Strategic Analysis*, vol.11, no.1, April 1987, 7. Rasul B. Rais, a very perceptive Pakistani scholar, agrees with the view that Pakistan is bound to lose if it embarks on nuclear weapons competition with India. He is, however, extremely sceptical about the theory that the existence of mutual nuclear deterrence between India and Pakistan would, as Subrahmanyam argues, establish the 'stability of deterrence' in the Indian subcontinent.

According to Rais, 'Because of its dependent and underdeveloped technological base, Pakistan essentially remains a static threshold nuclear power. Demonstrated capability to produce weapons-usable materials does not automatically lend Pakistan a credible nuclear status. The breakthrough in perfecting the centrifuge enrichment process at Kahuta does not reflect an overall technological change in critical areas of nuclear weapons capability. However, the possession of fissile materials opens up Pakistani options, and these would essentially be determined by the Indian nuclear decision-making. Naturally, any Pakistani attempt to acquire nuclear capability to neutralize an assumed Indian nuclear threat would prompt India to strive for a nuclear edge over its adversary by means of its advanced space programme, rocketry, and cumulative technological superiority. The Pakistani goals of a static geopolitical equilibrium in South Asia ... might be better served in the nuclear sphere by its presently perceived capability to produce fissile materials. The development of operational nuclear weapon systems in South Asia might not produce a stable strategic environment as advocated by the proponents of the bomb option in both India and Pakistan. The outdated NATO doctrine of massive retaliation and nuclear option to augment meager conventional defence sources is hardly relevant in Pakistan's case because of the vast and unbridgeable disparities in the conventional and assumed nuclear capabilities of the adversaries.' Rasul B. Rais, op. cit., 471–2.

5 Carnegie Task Force on Non-Proliferation and South Asian Security, *Nuclear Weapons and South Asian Security*, Carnegie Endowment for International Peace, Washington DC 1988, 56.

6 See 'India Tests Surface-to-Surface Missile', *International Herald Tribune*, 26 February 1988. According to this report, the missile that was tested was 'similar in design to the Soviet Scud missile, was about 35 feet (10 meters) high and fuelled by liquid propellant, and ... could be fired from a mobile launcher and hit a target up to 160 miles (260 kilometers) away'. The report also mentioned that, 'Military experts said that the missile could deliver nuclear warheads but that they believed that it would be used in conventional roles, such as attacking installations behind enemy lines.' For details of India's IRBM

development, see 'Agni: Chariot of Fire', *India Today*, 15 June 1989, 10–13. According to this report, 'armed with a nuclear warhead, Agni offers the potential to put India on par with China as far as military deterrence is concerned'. (p. 10)

7 For relevant details of Chinese nuclear weapons capability, see the section on 'Strategic Force Development and Deployment' in William T. Tow, 'China's Modernization and the Big Powers: Strategic Implications', in David M. Lampton and Caterine H. Keyser, op. cit, 172–7.

8 Jasjit Singh, 'Indian Security: a Framework for National Strategy', *Strategic Analysis*, vol.11, no.8, November 1987, 898. The recently retired Indian Chief of Army Staff, General K. Sundarji, who has had the reputation of being a 'thinking man's general', also emphasised the primacy of the Chinese threat to India over that posed by Pakistan. In an interview immediately after his retirement as the army chief, General Sundarji declared: 'Against China we are infinitely better prepared now, though there are a few soft areas. Against Pakistan, our dissuasive and riposte capabilities are good. Our major problem is going to be China. Pakistan we can take care of *en passant.*' 'General K. Sundarji: Disputed Legacy', *India Today*, 15 May 1988, 39.

9 Pradyot Pradhan, 'People's Republic of China: a Security Threat to India', *Strategic Analysis*, vol.11, no.10, January 1988, 1200.

10 K. Subrahmanyam, 'India's Security Challenges and Responses: Evolving a Security Doctrine', *Strategic Analysis*, vol.11, no.1, April 1987, 9.

11 ibid., 8.

12 K. Subrahmanyam, 'Indian Attitudes towards the NPT', in SIPRI, *Nuclear Proliferation Problems*, Almqvist and Wiksell, Stockholm, and MIT Press, Cambridge, Mass, 1974, 263, (italics in extract added).

13 A veteran Indian journalist is worth quoting in this context: 'The implicit nuclear umbrella provided by the Indo-Soviet treaty is in danger of springing leaks, with Mikhail Gorbachev's accelerated efforts to befriend China. This lends urgency to the need for reassessment of India's nuclear policy.' S. Nihal Singh, 'India: Neither Yes nor No to a Nuclear Deterrent', *International Herald Tribune*, 11 January 1988.

5

India, Indonesia, and Vietnam:
Coincidence of Interests?

It is in the light of these Indian perceptions of the projected increase in Chinese capabilities and the uncertainties surrounding Chinese intentions, that both Indochina and ASEAN have assumed added importance in terms of New Delhi's overall foreign policy concerns. These Indian perceptions have also had the effect of augmenting the centrality of roles traditionally prescribed by New Delhi for the pivotal countries in the two groupings – Vietnam and Indonesia – in its overall approach towards Southeast Asia and the empathy demonstrated by it towards the fundamental concerns of Indonesian and Vietnamese foreign policies.[1]

As far as New Delhi is concerned, this empathy is the result, at least in part, of the Indian admiration for the genuinely nationalist and anti-colonial credentials of the founding fathers of independent Indonesia and Vietnam. It is the result also of the Indian recognition that Indonesia and Vietnam, as regionally preeminent powers in archipelagic and mainland Southeast Asia respectively, share an important characteristic with India in terms of their regional status. Given India's own aspirations, as the preeminent power in the subcontinent, for a managerial role in its own region and for autonomy of action *vis-à-vis* the dominant global powers, its policy-makers have been normally sympathetic towards such aspirations harboured by similarly situated 'regional influentials' in general and Indonesia and Vietnam, the preeminent powers in non-Communist and Communist Southeast Asia respectively, in particular.

The combination of these two factors, – the impeccable anti-colonial credentials of the Indonesian and Vietnamese national movements and their similar status as preeminent regional powers interested in maintaining their position as autonomous decision-making centres in a world dominated by the superpowers – has led the Indian leaders to believe that these countries have not merely shared a common colonial past with India, but, more importantly, that as 'regional influentials' they share with it significant interests and aspirations with regard to the present and future workings of the international political system. This basic ingredient of the Indian perception of Indonesia and Vietnam has survived the numerous ups and downs in New Delhi's relations with both Jakarta and Hanoi.

India's positive view of Indonesia and Vietnam has been immeasurably strengthened by the various degrees of antipathy towards China shared by the three countries. This shared concern has, in fact, led to the Indian perception that Vietnam and Indonesia form the kingpins of any strategy aimed at preventing the expansion of Chinese influence in Southeast Asia. This Indian perception is buttressed by the fact that the Vietnamese and Indonesian antagonisms towards China are, if anything, based on even more solid historical foundations than is the case with India's attitude towards Beijing.

The Vietnamese have a centuries' old history of unrelenting struggle against Chinese attempts, sometimes successful, to dominate the region now known as Vietnam.[2] Although the North Vietnamese rulers were beholden to Communist China for the help rendered by the latter in their struggle first against the French and then against the Americans, this Chinese support did not come without a high price. On the one hand, it all but embroiled Vietnam in the Sino-Soviet ideological and political dispute and, on the other, it led to sustained Chinese pressure on Hanoi following the Sino-American rapprochement of 1971 to compromise, or at least delay the achievement of, its cherished objective of Vietnamese reunification under Communist rule. Finally, following Vietnam's refusal to toe the Chinese line after the fall of Saigon in 1975 and its determination to act as the managerial power in Communist Indochina, Beijing not merely extended support to the Kampuchean Khmer Rouge to defy Vietnamese wishes, it launched a punitive attack on Vietnam in February 1979 in retaliation for the Vietnamese invasion of Kampuchea in December 1978, which overthrew the Khmer Rouge and installed Heng Samrin in power in Phnom Penh.

The Chinese invasion of Vietnam particularly stirred anti-Chinese emotions in India for two reasons. First, it was launched while the then Indian Foreign Minister, A. B. Vajpayee, was on a visit to China, the first such visit in two decades. The timing of the attack was a source of great embarrassment for the Indian government and the minister had to cut short his visit as an act of protest. At that time, New Delhi, inflating its own importance in Chinese calculations, interpreted the timing as a deliberate Chinese attempt to spoil India's relations with Vietnam. Second, and more important, the Chinese invasion of Vietnam very strongly reminded policy-makers and opinion-moulders in New Delhi of the Chinese incursion into India across the Himalayas in October 1962, also ostensibly to teach India a 'lesson'. This Indian image was strengthened by the Chinese statements issued at the time of the Chinese invasion of Vietnam, which were almost identical to those issued by Beijing during the Sino-Indian border war.

Indonesian antipathy towards China, despite the aberration of Sukarno's last years, when Jakarta teamed up with Beijing to confront what Sukarno considered to be Anglo-American designs in Southeast Asia deleterious to Indonesian interests, runs almost as deep as that of Vietnam. Based primarily on the indigenous Indonesians' negative perceptions of the 'exploitative', affluent and often powerful Chinese minority in the country, it has been overlaid by the Indonesian ruling elite's strong aversion towards the Communist character of the Chinese regime. Beijing's attempt to intervene in Indonesian domestic affairs in the 1950s, using as a medium the issue of the status of overseas Chinese, was a strong reminder to Jakarta that a powerful and stable central authority in China could be easily tempted to utilize the Chinese minority in the country to advance its own objectives in the region.

Even more important, China's perceived role as the mentor of the Communist Party of Indonesia (PKI) and its alleged encouragement of the latter's strategy of a gradual takeover of the country under the guise of support for Sukarno's policies and by the exclusion of the military – Sukarno's other support base – from the effective exercise of power, totally alienated the military leadership from China as well as from the PKI. The abortive Communist coup of 1965 proved to be the proverbial last straw as far as the Indonesian military leadership was concerned, confirming as it did the military's worst apprehensions regarding Communist Chinese 'designs'. The breach in Indonesia's diplomatic relations with China that took place in the aftermath of the failed coup, and the takeover of power by the military under Suharto, has yet to be repaired. In the light of this background, it is not surprising that the Indonesian ruling elite considers China to be the primary source of external-cum-internal threat to Indonesia. Therefore, despite the fact that Jakarta continues to subscribe to the ASEAN consensus on the Kampuchean issue, the conflict in Indochina, particularly the Chinese punitive attack on Vietnam, has confirmed the predominant Indonesian perception that China poses the major threat to the Southeast Asian region as a whole.[3]

In view of these Vietnamese and Indonesian experiences with China as well as the other foreign policy concerns which they share with India, it would not be wrong to assume that, if there is an Indian 'grand design' about Southeast Asia, Indonesia and Vietnam form the two main pillars on which it is based. This does not mean that it has been smooth sailing all the way for India in terms of its relations with Vietnam and Indonesia. Reference has already been made to Indian reservations regarding the dominant strand of Vietnamese nationalism in the late 1940s and the early 1950s, because of the Communist-dominated character of the Vietminh during its fight for independence against the French, and the cordial relations between New Delhi and Saigon during the second half of the 1950s. In fact, even on the eve of the Geneva Conference of 1954 (which worked out a peace plan for Indochina and where India, in the person of Krishna Menon, was extremely active although in an unofficial capacity) when Nehru presented his own peace plan for Indochina, he called for a ceasefire but not for an immediate withdrawal of French troops from Indochina. This, as one Indian observer has put it, was related to India's anxiety 'in case the Communists overran the whole of Indochina'.[4] This interpretation is borne out by Krishna Menon's statement in the Upper House of the Indian Parliament on 18 May 1954 that, 'While it may be a piece of agreeable rhetoric to talk about the withdrawal of French troops from Indochina first, it is not practical politics'.[5]

President Diem's visit to India in November 1957 and the enthusiastic welcome accorded to him by the Indian government as 'the Head of a State, which like us has emerged as a free nation only recently after a long spell of foreign domination'[6] marked the high point in the development of a relatively warm relationship between Saigon and New Delhi.[7] Although India, as the chairman of the International Control Commission (ICC) for Vietnam, was under pressure to maintain an even-handed approach towards the two Vietnamese states, its stance in the late 1950s and the early 1960s, even within the Commission, was distinctly sympathetic to South Vietnam, to the great chagrin of Hanoi. This was in marked contrast to the situation from 1954 to 1956 when India's dealings, as chairman of the ICC, with Hanoi were very smooth compared to the rough time it had in its relationship with the authorities in Saigon, who deliberately obstructed the functioning of the ICC and even allowed mobs to attack its headquarters.

While the change in the New Delhi attitude from the late 1950s onwards towards the two Vietnamese entities could in part be related to deteriorating Sino-Indian relations, it was even more a function of India's unfavourable reaction to Hanoi's attempt to subvert the Saigon regime through infiltration and guerrilla warfare. As one author has put it, 'India's policy, whether in India or elsewhere, was consistently opposed to the imposition of Communism from outside, especially through subversion.'[8] That the concern with the China factor was secondary is borne out by the fact that it was not until the outbreak of the Sino-Indian border war in October–November 1962 that North Vietnam came out in open support of China in the latter's dispute with India. India, on the other hand, had joined Canada as early as June 1962 in a majority report of the ICC condemning Hanoi's role in the subversion of South Vietnam, thereby handing Saigon and its external supporters a major propaganda victory.

The increasing unpopularity and the shrinking base of the Saigon regime in the 1960s plus direct American involvement in the war against the NLF and North Vietnam tilted the balance of Indian sympathies once again in favour of Hanoi during the second half of the 1960s and thereafter. However, this tilt did not come about without considerable soul-searching and internal debate among India's foreign policy-makers, especially in the context of the Sino-Indian border war of 1962 and the continuing suspicion of Communist North Vietnam's subversive designs. As one Indian specialist on Southeast Asia has pointed out, even after America's direct involvement in the Vietnam War, 'In some quarters in New Delhi it was mistakenly held that

America was doing the job in Southeast Asia for us, namely taming the Chinese power. Nothing could be more thoughtless and unimaginative.'[9]

The North Vietnamese attempt during the second half of the 1960s and the first half of the 1970s to maintain equidistance, as far as possible, from both Beijing and Moscow, India's increasingly warm relationship with the latter (particularly in the context of the Sino-Soviet dispute), and the realization that Hanoi's support to Beijing was tactical rather than strategic and that the situation could be reversed if Hanoi had the option to do so, all contributed to the change in New Delhi's perception of North Vietnam and a return to its earlier stance of the 1954–6 period, which had been more sympathetic to Hanoi than to Saigon. However, it is worth noting that India recognized the Democratic Republic of Vietnam (DRV) only in January 1972 and that this act was directly linked to Indian ire over the American decision to deploy a naval task force led by the aircraft carrier *USS Enterprise* in the Bay of Bengal during the Indo-Pakistani war in December 1971 as a demonstration of American support to Pakistan and as a warning signal, however ineffective, to India.

Similarly, Indian relations with Indonesia ran into difficulties during the last years of the Sukarno era. During that period the divergent Indian and the Indonesian perceptions of the role of the Non-Aligned Movement in an essentially bipolar world, their widely different views regarding the convening of a 'second Bandung conference' of Afro-Asian states and of its prospective membership, the Indonesian leader's perception of his country's role in the Indian Ocean, Jakarta's alignment with Beijing as a part of its 'grand strategy' to combat 'imperialism', India's support for the idea of a Malaysian federation and its subsequent tilt in favour of Kuala Lumpur during the period of the *konfrontasi* and, in retaliation, the Indonesian political and military support to Pakistan in its confrontation with India over Kashmir, all added up to a relatively tense atmosphere in the bilateral relations between the two countries.[10] The divergent stances adopted by Nehru and Sukarno at the First Non-Aligned Summit in Belgrade in September 1961 on anti-colonialism on the one hand and the importance of world peace in a nuclear age on the other, symbolized the beginning of overt deterioration in Indo-Indonesian relations – a process that culminated in the

1963–5 period, which included the Indian moral support to Malaysia in its confrontation with Indonesia and the latter's moral and material support to Pakistan during the India–Pakistan war of September 1965.[11]

That the Indonesian assistance to Pakistan could have led to a direct military confrontation between Indian and Indonesia is borne out by the testimony of a leading expert of Indian naval power, Raju Thomas. According to him, 'Despite the Indian navy's non-participation [in the India–Pakistan war of 1965], some reports indicate that there might have been an Indonesian naval threat during the war. President Sukarno, who had recently acquired a US $1 billion navy from the Soviet Union, had made vague threats to intercede on the Pakistan side. Later, Pakistan's Air Marshal Asghar Khan revealed in his memoirs that Sukarno had in fact offered to divert Indian attention from Pakistan by seizing the Andaman and Nicobar islands in the Bay of Bengal.'[12] The same author has further asserted that, 'Although the Pakistani naval threat was never substantial, naval threats have been perceived [by India] previously from Indonesia under Sukarno and from Iran under the Shah, whose states had substantial numbers of imposing combat vessels. However, since the fall of both leaders, Indonesian and Iranian naval forces have declined and show no tendency of further development that would seriously threaten the Indian navy. In spite of these favourable conditions, the potential for growth by the Pakistani, Indonesian, and Iranian navies is still perceived as considerable, especially because all three states possess either substantial foreign exchange reserves or have access to such income. All three states also have the capacity to train efficient and capable naval manpower.'[13]

Much of the damage done to Indo-Indonesian relations during the last years of the Sukarno era was repaired following the coming to power of the 'New Order' regime in Jakarta. A flurry of ministerial visits on both sides, and particularly the efforts of the then Indonesian Foreign Minister, Adam Malik, did much to restore relations to a more even keel. Adam Malik even demonstrated a degree of empathy for India's treaty relationship with the Soviet Union. This was testified by a remark he made in 1972, in the context of the Indonesian decision to turn down a Soviet offer of a Treaty of Peace and Friendship on the lines of the Indo-Soviet Treaty, that 'We have no need for a treaty like that now. *Our need is not the same as*

41

India's.[14] It is interesting to note that the momentum for bilateral discussions built up in the early days of the Suharto regime has been maintained through the last two decades with periodic discussions between the two countries held regularly ranging from the Foreign Ministers' level to meetings between delegations of the Indonesian Centre for Strategic and International Studies and the Indian Institute for Defence Studies and Analyses.

Despite these exchanges and the generally cordial atmosphere currently surrounding Indian–Indonesian relations, Indonesian suspicions of Indian 'designs' have not totally disappeared. These suspicions are related partially to the divergent Indian and Indonesian perceptions of the two superpowers, especially to Indonesia's residual mistrust, a legacy of the abortive Communist coup of 1965, of the Soviet Union, which continues to be India's major arms supplier, a role it had once performed for Sukarno's Indonesia. However, more importantly, they are the products of geographic proximity of India to Indonesian, particularly of India's island territories of Andaman and Nicobar in the Bay of Bengal, which are barely 90 miles from the Straits of Malacca and literally next door to the Indonesia island of Sumatra. Indonesian concerns about Indian intentions have been recently heightened by India's attempts to augment its naval power and acquire a power projection capability in the vicinity of the subcontinent.[15]

Certain military circles in Indonesia were particularly disturbed by press reports in 1986 that India was planning to build a major naval base on Great Nicobar island, separated from northern Sumatra by only 160 kilometres. Particular note was taken in Indonesia of an article in the *Far Eastern Economic Review* of 15 May 1986 which mentioned that the Indian decision to build this base 'underlines India's drive for a multi-role blue water navy' in the vicinity of the Straits of Malacca.[16] When queried on the subject at a press conference, the then Indonesian Foreign Minister, while confirming that India was building a base as reported, quickly added that it was 'an Indian affair' and that if circumstances permitted Indonesia would also in turn build a base on the island of Rando, which is the nearest point to Nicobar.[17] The *Far Eastern Economic Review* article quoted above had also stated that, 'Work on the Nicobar runway has actually been suspended for an indefinite period for unexplained reasons. Officials will not say whether it has anything to do with unofficial Indonesian objections to the project'.[18]

My own conversations in New Delhi during a visit to the Indian capital in May–June 1987 gave me the distinct impression that while Indonesian unease might have been a contributing factor to the Indian decision to shelve the Great Nicobar base project, the primary consideration was financial. Given the constraints on defence-spending and the security priorities of the Indian government, New Delhi apparently came to the conclusion that the financial layout on the base would far exceed the returns in terms of buying greater security for the country. It seems that, even in terms of the Indian Navy's own priorities, expenditure on a static base in the Bay of Bengal was not considered as cost-effective as the acquisition of greater naval mobility and the capacity to deter hostile action against the island territories by bringing to bear greater 'floating power' in case of a confrontation around these territories, whether in the Bay of Bengal or in the Arabian Sea.

Moreover, as was explained to me by a very high source in the Indian Navy, the Andaman and Nicobar islands faced no threats in the foreseeable future, especially since India's maritime boundaries with all its Southeast Asian neighbours — Burma, Thailand, and Indonesia — have been amicably demarcated[19] and there are no disputes that require a permanent naval presence in the island territories. This Indian decision also fits in with the currently dominant doctrine in the Indian Navy that India's naval strategy should be based on 'floating' sea-control capability, a task best performed by aircraft carriers and other large surface vessels which do not come cheap, supplemented by a 'sea-denial' capability based on the acquisition of modern submarines. The navy would, therefore, like to use the financial resources allocated to it for the acquisition of greater sea-control and sea-denial capability rather than fritter them away on fixed island bases which have only limited value in terms of the projection of naval and air power over the vast expanses of the Indian Ocean. The recent Indian acquisition of a nuclear-powered submarine from the Soviet Union also fits in with the overall strategy of investing in 'floating power' rather than in fixed bases in its island territories.[20]

In this context, Indonesian objections, even if expressed unofficially, would seem to have supplemented the Indian navy's own lukewarm attitude towards a base in Great Nicobar, especially if it was to be built at the expense of more pressing naval needs. In fact, I was informed by very high level sources that the Chief of the Indian Naval Staff had invited the Indonesian naval chief to visit India and would have liked to take the latter on a tour of the Andaman and Nicobar islands to show him what the Indians were, or were not, doing in the island territories in the vicinity of Indonesia and the Straits of Malacca.

However, at least some elements within the Indonesian military continue to be worried about both India's expanding naval and air power projection capabilities and its links with the Soviet Union. This became evident when, on the eve of the Indian Prime Minister's visit to Jakarta in October 1986, General Harsudiyono Hartas, the Indonesian general commanding the elite Diponegoro Command and a former commander of Northern Sumatra from 1983 to 1985, 'hinted that Soviet submarines were roaming in Indonesian waters around Sabang, the northern tip of Sumatra, and indicated that the submarines had come from the Indian base on Nicobar Island. Sabang faces the Andaman group of islands in the Bay of Bengal to its north and the entrance to the strategic Straits of Malacca to its east.'[21]

The Indian reaction to General Hartas's statement was swift and sharp. New Delhi, both in its protest made to the Indonesian Ambassador in India and at the press conference by the Indian Ambassador in Jakarta on the eve of Rajiv Gandhi's visit, denied that there was either a naval base in Nicobar or that any foreign power was using it. As a result of the sharp Indian reaction, the Indonesian Foreign Ministry issued a statement down-playing the issue and taking the position that General Hartas's remarks had been taken 'out of context'. It went on to say: 'It is true that many submarines (Soviet or otherwise) pass through Indonesian waters, but they do not transgress new international sea laws which provide for the right of international passage through the straits.'[22] Despite this diplomatic exercise on Indonesia's part aimed at defusing the issue so as not to spoil the atmosphere at the time of the Indian Prime Minister's visit to Jakarta, the incident left a lingering feeling that General Hartas's remarks 'reflected a long-standing, but well-hidden, concern within Indonesian security circles about India's relationship with the Soviet Union'.[23]

The Indian acquisition on lease in early 1988 of a Charlie class nuclear-powered submarine from the Soviet Union for training purposes has, it seems, added to regional, including Indonesian, concerns about India's expanding naval power projection capabilities. Their unease has been heightened especially as a result of the speculation that this is but the prelude to the outright acquisition by India in 1991 of the first of four Soviet nuclear-powered Sierra class hunter-killer submarines. Furthermore, it makes India the sixth country to have acquired a nuclear-powered submarine — the others being the United States, the Soviet Union, the United Kingdom, France and China — and, if followed up by the acquisition of the Sierra class submarines, could 'give India the requisite muscle to ensure its strategic interests were recognized by world powers.'[24]

The acquisition of a second aircraft carrier by the Indian navy, had in fact, raised hackles as far afield as Australia.[25] This Australian concern was augmented by the Indian acquisition of a nuclear-powered submarine from the Soviet Union for training purposes. While inaugurating a seminar on 'Australia and the Indian Ocean' in Fremantle, Western Australia, on 28 March 1988, the Australian Defence Minister, Kim Beazley, called the expansion of Indian naval capabilities 'intriguing'. While ruling out a direct Indian threat to Australia, Beazley stated that 'Any development of a force projection capability in our general region must interest us.... In India's case, the possession of a substantial number of carriers, the possibility of balanced carrier battle groups and submarines, poses possibilities for extensively increased Indian influence at the major eastern Indian Ocean choke points. We are active in defence undertakings in this area and will watch diplomatic developments carefully.' At the same seminar former Australian Senator Peter Sim, who had been chairman of the Joint Committee on Foreign Affairs and Defence of the Australian Parliament for several years in the 1970s and the early 1980s, declared, with more emotion than knowledge, that 'The Indian navy will be in a position, by the end of the century, to dominate the Indian Ocean. This build up is causing concern to regional countries stretching from Africa to Indonesia and Thailand.... The projection capabilities of the Indian force provide visible evidence of Indian aspirations to achieve politico-military predominance in the Indian Ocean.'[26]

Such concern is bound to increase in the light of two other reports appearing in the first half of 1988. The first of these was the statement made by the British Secretary of State for Defence, George Younger, in January 1988 in New Delhi that 'Britain [which recently supplied India its second aircraft carrier for US $35 million] was also ready to offer designs of nuclear-powered and Invincible-class aircraft carriers to India, which is planning to build its third carrier on its own by 1992.'[27]

The second report, attributed to the Press Trust of India (PTI), appeared in April 1988. It stated that, as part of its naval build up, India had received long-range reconnaissance aircraft that would allow it to scour the Indian Ocean from South Africa to Australia. PTI quoted official Indian sources as saying that the first batch of TU-142 maritime reconnaissance aircraft (designated 'Bear' by NATO), consisting of not more than four planes, was recently delivered to India by the Soviet Union. It was to be formally inducted into the Indian navy on 16 April 1988 and would be based in Goa on India's west coast. Powered by four turboprops, the TU-142 can fly at 800 kmh and has a range of more than 11,000 km. An independent defence analyst, explaining that the aircraft's main use would be for maritime reconnaissance and anti-submarine warfare, declared that, 'This gives the Indian navy perhaps the most dramatic means to know exactly what is happening in the seas around India and well away. If you want to build up a navy with a lot of punch, you need eyes and ears, and this is exactly what you are getting.... The biggest attribute of the Bear is its fantastic endurance. It can take off from a coastal airfield and fly to South Africa and back.' He went on to say that the plane could also reach the west coast of Australia on missions across the Indian Ocean. The Indian acquisition of these aircraft would, reportedly, leave only the US navy with a greater reconnaissance capability in the Indian Ocean.[28]

Indian strategists, however, argue that the acquisition of a respectable naval surveillance and power projection capability by New Delhi is a must, among other things, because of the expansion of Chinese naval capabilities in recent years. According to one Indian observer, 'The Chinese development of SLBM force and the possibility in the near future that it may cruise into the Indian Ocean ... poses grave security threats to India. The contingency puts forth immediate concern for New Delhi and forces her to develop a reasonable deterrence in the form of anti-submarine warfare (ASW) capabilities (including aircraft carrier for this role) and development and possession of submarines.'[29]

The Indian attempt to acquire such 'deterrent' capabilities *vis-à-vis* China, unfortunately, raises suspicions among its neighbours, particularly Indonesia, that these very capabilities could be used by India to dominate the subcontinent's extended maritime environment which includes much of the seas around Southeast Asia. It would, then, according to this logic, be just a short step for India to attempt to dominate archipelagic, if not mainland, Southeast Asia. Such a position, Indian analysts argue, fails to take into account the fact that the preeminent naval presence in the Indian Ocean is that of the United States with France, the United Kingdom, and the Soviet Union also maintaining significant naval capabilities in the Indian subcontinent's maritime environment. According to them, these external presences rule out any hypothetical Indian domination of the Indian Ocean.

However, despite the fact that such suspicions surface periodically and tend to cast shadows on Indian–Indonesian relations, there seems to be a clear understanding within the policy-making circles in New Delhi that there is a basic convergence of Indian and Indonesian interests in relation to Southern Asia and the Indian Ocean region that should not be lost sight of while dealing with, what New Delhi considers, 'temporary aberrations' that crop up in the bilateral relations of the two countries. Indian policy-makers also assume, one could argue on the basis of insufficient evidence, that this attitude is reciprocated in Jakarta's long-term view of India and of the importance of Indo-Indonesian relations. This optimistic Indian assumption regarding Indonesia's long-term attitude and policy towards India seems to emerge, at least partly, from the reasoning that, 'Some of the early successes of Indonesian foreign policy were based on close cooperation with India.... Only through a revival of this element can Indonesia project its influence beyond the confines of the southern part of Southeast Asia.'[30]

This assumption, however, could turn out to be erroneous particularly if India's technological, and, therefore, military capabilities, especially those related to air and naval power projection, continue to outrun Indonesian capabilities and if the technological gap between the two countries continues to widen steadily. This process could end up augmenting Indonesian fears of Indian 'designs', even though these apprehensions would be based not so much on Indian intentions as on Indian capabilities. That this could well be the case is borne out by Raju Thomas's conclusion in his study of Indian security policy that, 'The increasing technological momentum will have significant spillover effects on the growth of India's conventional and potential nuclear weapons capabilities... [especially since] the growth of Indian military capabilities is, to a certain extent, unrelated to Indian threat perceptions and tends to be an autonomous trend based on civilian technological growth. The situation is similar to that found in the United States, where advances in technology often define defence needs. In effect, India's extended strategic interests in the Middle East, Southeast Asia, and the Indian Ocean arise as much from India's growing military reach, based on autonomous arms build-up, as from perceptions of indirect threats prevailing in distant theatres of war that may affect the subcontinent. Technological growth, therefore, has made India into a regional power that may rival China in the future.'[31]

It would be equally wrong to assume, however, that Indonesian attitudes towards India are likely to be determined exclusively, or even primarily, by Jakarta's concerns regarding the expansion of India's power projection capabilities. There are many important factors, both political and economic, that could move the two countries towards closer cooperation in the future. In fact, the political rationale for increased economic cooperation between New Delhi and Jakarta was most eloquently expressed by the then Indonesian Minister of Industry, A. R. Soehoed, at an Indo-Indonesian seminar held in January 1982. The Indonesian minister, while comparing the respective merits of the concepts of the 'Pacific Community' and the 'Indian Ocean Community', stated frankly that the latter concept 'interests us more'. In this context, he went on to say that there was much that India and Indonesia could do to advance mutual economic and technical cooperation as a nucleus for an 'Indian Ocean Community'. He concluded that, 'In the struggle for a better place in the sun for the third world, the odds for building the Indian Ocean Community may turn out to be much better than for the Pacific Community. For in the former the cooperative relationships would be in the interest of developing countries bordering the Ocean. In the latter, where the leading proponents are industrialized countries, there is the contingent risk that it will perpetuate the existing North–South trading pattern. Besides, the reality of China and the Soviet Union validly claiming to be Pacific Basin countries, constitutes an inherent destabilizing presence, whether or not they are invited and willing to join the Pacific Community.'[32]

In addition to these general factors mentioned by the former Indonesian minister, India and Indonesia have on occasion demonstrated that their policies towards some regional issues tend to run on parallel, if not identical, lines. This has been nowhere as clear as in relation to the Kampuchean issue which involved for both New Delhi and Jakarta the crucial questions of their relationship with Hanoi on the one hand and their suspicions of China on the other. Therefore, it is appropriate that in the next chapter we turn to a discussion of Indian policy on the Kampuchean issue.

Notes

1 That this is not a new phenomenon and that Indian strategic analysts were aware of the beneficial effects of a tripartite coordination of Indian, Indonesian, and Vietnamese capabilities, particularly in the context of the British decision in the late 1960s to withdraw from 'east of Suez', is borne out by the analysis in K. Subrahmanyam's article 'The Ebb and Flow of Power in the Indian Ocean Area', published in January–March 1968 issue of *USI Journal* (New Delhi). The concluding paragraph of this article reads as follows: 'The withdrawal of the British forces from Malaysia and Singapore is only a belated recognition of the limitations on the British power in the post-colonial era and not likely to have any impact on the strategic balance in South-East Asia. The projection of US naval power and the Soviet naval power into the Indian Ocean is of great political significance, but strategically they are likely to be mutually deterrent. *The expansion of Indian naval power, the revival of Indonesian power and growth of Vietnamese navy – if that is possible – are likely to result in a multi-polar local balance in South-East Asia and provide strong countervailing influence to Chinese expansionism in Asia, if it occurs. The Japanese and Australian navies may add to this countervailing influence.*' (p. 14, italics added).

2 For a balanced analysis of the conflict between China and Vietnam, see William J. Duiker, *China and Vietnam: the Roots of Conflict*, Institute of Southeast Asian Studies, University of California, Berkeley, 1986. Duiker arrives at the following conclusion in his book: 'In actuality ... even the rivalry over influence in Indochina is only a surface manifestation of a deeper issue dividing the two countries.

Behind the Cambodian dispute is the broader problem of placing Sino-Vietnamese relations on a new footing with the end of the Vietnam War in 1975. China ... appears determined to restore its traditional role in Southeast Asia by creating a string of submissive client states along its southern frontier. Vietnam ... is equally determined to reassert its independence and realize its own national destiny.' (pp.116–17). He goes on to assert: 'If this analysis is correct, it is unlikely that there will be a major breakthrough in Sino-Vietnamese relations in the near future.' (p. 121).

3 For a perceptive discussion of this subject by an Indonesian scholar, see J. Soedjati Djiwandono, 'The Soviet Presence in the Asia–Pacific Region: an Indonesian Perspective', *Indonesian Quarterly*, vol.12, no.4, October 1984, 428. The author buttresses his argument that China, not Vietnam, is considered the main source of threat to Southeast Asia by the Indonesian government, by referring to statements by General Murdani, Commander of the Indonesian Armed Forces, on his visit to Vietnam (*The Nation*, 24 February 1984), and by President Suhartoc *Straits Times* and *Bangkok Post*, 28 February 1984) (see Djiwandono, p. 428, Footnote 11).

Another leading Indonesian scholar, Hadi Soesastro, has also written in the same vein: 'In fact, in terms of threat perceptions in the region, the Soviet Union is seen as a more distant threat than the PRC. Perceptions after all, are created through a set of beliefs about intentions as well as of calculations about capabilities. China would seem a greater threat insofar as the set of beliefs about intentions is concerned; if, however, one were to judge by the set of calculations about capabilities, the Soviets would seem a greater threat....On the whole ASEAN is rather relaxed in facing the potential Soviet menace, which is considered to be largely military.... It is believed that if the Soviets enter the region in a degree as to endanger Southeast Asia, it would be Chinese provocations that would have to answer for it.' Hadi Soesastro, 'Contemporary Global Situation and Rising Tensions', in K. Subrahmanyam (ed.), *India, Indonesia, and the New Cold War*, Institute for Defence Studies and Analyses, New Delhi, 1984, 30–1.

4 Parimal Kumar Das, *India and the Vietnam War*, Young Asia Publications, New Delhi, 1972, 22.

5 Quoted in ibid., 22.

6 The statement is from Indian President Rajendra Prasad's banquet speech in honour of President Diem on 5 November 1957. It is quoted in D. R. Sardesai, *Indian Foreign Policy in Cambodia, Laos, and Vietnam, 1947–1964*, University of California Press, Berkeley and Los Angeles, 1968, p. 107.

7 President Ho Chi Minh of the Democratic Republic of Vietnam also paid an official visit to India in February 1958, shortly after the visit by President Diem of South Vietnam.

8 D. R. Sardesai, op cit., 201. For details of India's position in the ICC during the early 1960s, see Sardesai, pp. 201–9.

9 Parimal Kumar Das, op. cit., 5.

10 For a thorough review of Indo-Indonesian relations during this difficult period in their bilateral relationship, see B. D. Arora,

Indian-Indonesian Relations (1961–1980), Asian Educational Services, New Delhi, 1981, chapters 2 to 6.

11 For details, see Kirdi Dipoyudo, 'Indonesia-India Bilateral Relations', *Indonesian Quarterly*, vol.13, no.4, October 1985, 509–23.

12 Raju G. C. Thomas, *Indian Security Policy*, Princeton University Press, Princeton, 1986, 152–3.

13 ibid., 173.

14 Quoted in G. V. C. Naidu, 'The Soviet Union and Southeast Asia', *Strategic Analysis*, vol.10, no.9, December 1986, 1092, (italics in extract added).

15 Such concerns about the expansion of the Indian Navy's role from one of coastal defence to one of power-projection in the waters in the vicinity of the subcontinent have been expressed not only by India's neighbours but also by bigger powers, which perceive India as poaching in their domain. However, the logic for this role expansion had been spelt out by K. M. Panikkar more than four decades ago. According to Panikkar, 'A navy is not meant for the defence of the coast. The coast has to be defended from the land. The object of a navy is to secure control of an area of the sea, thus preventing enemy ships from approaching the coast or interfering with trade and commerce and conversely after securing the control to blockade the enemy's coast and destroy his shipping. So a navy merely based on the coast degenerates into a subordinate wing of the army. The Indian navy whether it be large or small must learn this lesson. *Its purpose is to protect the seas and not the land and if it cannot protect the seas vital to India's defence then it is better not to have a navy at all.*' K. M. Panikkar, *India and the Indian Ocean: an Essay on the Influence of Sea Power on Indian History*, George Allen & Unwin, London, 1945, 96–7, (italics added).

16 Mohan Ram, 'Ruling the Waves: New Indian Base Extends Move Towards More Sea Power', *Far Eastern Economic Review*, 15 May 1986, 30.

17 *Indonesian Times*, 21 June 1986, quoted in Institute for Defence Studies and Analyses, *News Review on Southeast Asia*, July 1986, 435.

18 Mohan Ram, op. cit., 31.

19 The last of the maritime boundary agreements to be signed was with Burma. It was ratified in September 1987 during the visit of Burmese Foreign Minister Ye Gaung to New Delhi. The treaty 'delineates the exclusive economic zones of the two countries in the Andaman Sea by a single continuous line running across the Bay of Bengal and further south into the Andaman Sea. The dividing line is based on the principle of equidistance.... With the Burmese treaty, the only unsettled Indian Maritime borders are with Pakistan and Bangladesh.' Salamat Ali, 'Hands Across the Sea', *Far Eastern Economic Review*, 8 October 1987, 52. India's maritime boundaries with Thailand and Indonesia were delineated in a trilateral agreement signed in New Delhi in 1978.

20 However, given the constraints on India's resources there is an obvious tension between the navy's demands for a credible 'sea-control' capability on the one hand and its demands for a tangible 'sea-denial' capability on the other, especially since the potential

targets/adversaries for the two tasks are vastly different in terms of their counter-capabilities. For, as Ashley J. Tellis has argued, the Indian navy seeks to maintain 'sea control *vis-à-vis* the *regional navies* while simultaneously attaining a sea denial capability *vis-à-vis* the *external powers* in the Indian Ocean. The logic of naval technology has created substantially different force architectures for facilitating these contrasting missions .... Balancing these antinomous missions represents a *pons asinorum* for the Indian Navy.' Tellis goes on to argue that, 'Additional aircraft carriers are not optimal for the sea denial mission being considered against the external powers, and may also contribute negatively to Indian security by causing panic among India's neighbors and, thus, precipitate explicit alliances invoking the protection of foreign naval forces.' Ashley J. Tellis, 'India's Naval Expansion: Reflections on History and Strategy', *Comparative Strategy*, vol.6, no.2, 1987, 213–14, (italics added). Tellis' last point is borne out to some extent by Indonesian and Australian reactions to the expansion of Indian naval capabilities.

21 *Straits Times*, 13 October 1986.

22 ibid.

23 ibid.

24 Adam Keller, 'Regional Concern over India's N-Sub', *Straits Times*, 26 February 1988.

25 A. W. Gazebrook, 'India's Mounting Military Might', *Pacific Defence Reporter*, September 1986, 18–20.

26 Kim Beazley, 'The Two Ocean Navy' and Peter Sim, 'The Indian Ocean: Historical and Future Perspectives'. Papers presented to the seminar on 'Australia and the Indian Ocean' held in Fremantle, Western Australia, 28–30 March 1988.

27 'Britain Offers Military Package to India', *Straits Times*, 12 January 1988.

28 *Sunday Times* (Singapore), 10 April 1988.

29 Pradyot Pradhan, 'People's Republic of China: a Security Threat to India', *Strategic Analysis*, vol.11, no.10, January 1988, 1205.

30 Vishal Singh, 'ASEAN and the Security of Southeast Asia', *International Studies*, vol.23, no.3, July–September 1986, 219.

31 Raju, G. C. Thomas, op. cit., 291–2.

32 A. R. Soehoed, 'Economic and Technological Cooperation between India and Indonesia', in K. Subrahmanyam (ed.) *India, Indonesia, and the New Cold War*, Institute for Defence Studies and Analyses, New Delhi, 1984, 183.

6

India and the Kampuchean Issue

Despite the ups and downs in India's relations with both Indonesia and Vietnam, and despite the potential sources of tension particularly in the case of Indo-Indonesian relations, this background of shared interests, both in relation to China and to other issues, explains India's empathy for Vietnamese and Indonesian foreign policy concerns. In Indian perceptions it also explains what New Delhi considers the similarity in Indian and Indonesian attitudes towards Vietnam in relation to the Kampuchean problem. While Indian policy, especially since the return of the late Indira Gandhi to power in January 1980, has been openly sympathetic to Hanoi's Kampuchean dilemma, the Indonesian stance, although constrained by the ASEAN consensus on this issue, is viewed in New Delhi as far more flexible than that of the other members of ASEAN.

According to Indian policy-makers, the flexibility of the Indonesian position, like the understanding displayed by its Indian counterpart, is the result of Jakarta's appreciation of Vietnamese difficulties on the one hand and its perception of Hanoi as the major bulwark against Chinese expansionism in mainland Southeast Asia on the other. The comings and goings between Hanoi and Jakarta, including visits by such important Indonesian personalities as the former Armed Forces Chief and current Defence Minister, General Benny Murdani, and the former Foreign Minister, Mochtar Kusumaatmadja, as well as repeated Indonesian attempts, like the proposal for a 'cocktail party' of all Cambodian protagonists, to find common ground between Vietnam and ASEAN on the Kampuchean issue, testify to the Indonesian concern that continuing differences between

ASEAN and Vietnam on Kampuchea, and the consequent non-resolution of the problem, redounds only to the benefit of Beijing and its Kampuchean clients, the Khmer Rouge.[1]

The Indonesian position on the threat to non-Communist Southeast Asia posed by Vietnam and by Vietnam's alliance with the Soviet Union, which has resulted in Moscow acquiring bases in that country, was put in forthright terms by the then Foreign Minister Mochtar Kusumaatmadja in April 1986 on the eve of US President Ronald Reagan's visit to Indonesia. Mochtar stated very clearly that he saw no threat to Indonesia from Vietnam or from the Soviet base at Cam Ranh Bay. He went on to say: 'We are non-aligned and we feel that if America can have base facilities in the Philippines, there should be no objection to the Russians having them in Vietnam. It's no threat to us. Communism never came to us in big ships. Big bases and big warships are manifestations of big power rivalry, whether Communist or not.' On the threat to Southeast Asia posed by the Vietnamese occupation of Kampuchea, Mochtar was equally blunt: 'We feel that the Vietnamese no longer have the capability to destabilize. If they have difficulty in digesting Kampuchea, which after all is not so big a country, why should we worry so much?'[2]

Similarly, Indonesians do not think that Vietnam's superpower ally, the Soviet Union, poses a direct military threat either to Indonesia or to ASEAN as a whole. A leading Indonesian analyst of international affairs, Soedjati Djiwandono, has argued that talk of a direct military threat to ASEAN from the Soviet Union is far fetched. According to him, 'Such a suggestion is erroneous on at least two counts. Firstly, it confuses Soviet military capabilities with Soviet intentions. In point of fact, the US military forces at their bases in the Philippines are no less capable of doing the same job, for that matter. Secondly, it ignores the differences in national perceptions of threats.... [Furthermore] the terminology very often used in discussions about the Soviet presence in the Asia–Pacific region, such as the need to "counter" the Soviet advance, to "redress" the balance of power, to "halt" Soviet "expansionism", and to "meet" Soviet "threat" seems to be loaded with prejudice. It constantly puts the Soviet Union on the active side of the game, always taking the initiatives, with the rest of the region, particularly the United States, always reacting. The reality, of course, is not all that simple. It is not always easy to say for certain who reacts to who, who balances who, and who challenges who?'[3]

The Indian position on Kampuchea after the Vietnamese invasion in December 1978 evolved gradually, beginning with a non-committal and even-handed approach under the Janata Party government of Morarji Desai (that had come to power in March 1977), which did not recognize the DK (Democratic Kampuchea government of the Khmer Rouge ousted by the Vietnamese invasion) or the PRK (People's Republic of Kampuchea installed by the Vietnamese in Phnom Penh) government, and reaching its culmination with the recognition of Heng Samrin's PRK regime in July 1980 by Indira Gandhi's Congress (Indira) government which had been returned to office in January of the same year. The Janata policy was based on the premise that Indian foreign policy under Indira Gandhi, especially between 1969 and 1977, had tilted heavily in favour of the Soviet Union and its allies, thereby subverting India's declared policy of non-alignment. Morarji Desai and his Foreign Minister, A. B. Vajpayee, argued that India's policy had to be shifted back to one of 'genuine non-alignment' as between the two superpowers. Additionally, the Janata government was committed to the improvement of the country's relations with all its neighbours, especially since its leaders, when in opposition, had criticized Indira Gandhi for being insensitive to the interests and requirements of India's neighbours. A more friendly and positive approach towards China fitted in well with both these objectives of India's new leaders. On the one hand, it demonstrated that they were distancing themselves from the Soviet policy towards China and, on the other, it displayed their intention of pursuing a policy of 'good neighbourliness' towards India's largest neighbour. Not taking sides on the Kampuchean issue was, therefore, both a signal to China that India was aware of Chinese sensitivities on this issue as well as a dramatic demonstration of New Delhi's independence of Moscow.

While the Chinese attack on Vietnam in February 1979 had changed the perceptions of the Janata government to some degree and begun the Indian tilt towards Hanoi on Kampuchea, New Delhi, by and large, continued to maintain its even-handed approach on the problem till the end of 1979. Although Morarji Desai had been replaced by Charan Singh as prime minister by the time the Sixth Non-Aligned Summit was held in Havana in

September 1979, this did not signify any change in New Delhi's stand on the issue. When the controversial question of Kampuchean representation was raised at the Havana Summit, India adopted the position that the seat be kept vacant. Similarly, at the beginning of the 34th UN General Assembly session in late September 1979, India voted against seating the DK delegation without supporting its replacement by the representatives of the Heng Samrin regime.[4] Therefore, as an Indian analyst has concluded, in the final analysis, under both Morarji Desai and Charan Singh, the Indian government 'was critical both of the Chinese invasion of Vietnam and of the presence of the Vietnamese troops in Kampuchea, though it was more emphatic in its condemnation of the former than of the latter. It recognized the right neither of Pol Pot nor of Heng Samrin to represent Kampuchea.'[5]

Indira Gandhi's perspective on Southeast Asia in general, and Indochina in particular, was much more steeped in *realpolitik* than that of her immediate predecessors. As one author has put it, 'Indira Gandhi was determined to establish India as the preeminent power in South Asia.... Gandhi realized that if India were to become the paramount power in South Asia it would have to prevent a Chinese advance into Southeast Asia. From Gandhi's perspective, if Beijing succeeded in breaking Hanoi's will and in restoring its Khmer Rouge clients to power in Kampuchea, China would be in a much stronger position to contest Indian preeminence in South Asia. On the other hand, a strong, anti-Chinese Indochina would guard the flank of the Indian sphere of influence in South Asia. There was thus a convergence of Vietnamese and Indian views. Both were concerned with checking the southern advance of Chinese power.'[6] More than anything else, the Indian policy of recognition of the Heng Samrin-led PRK government emerged out of this convergence of Indian and Vietnamese interests as perceived by Indira Gandhi and her advisers. The near-consensus in Indian political circles on the recognition of the Heng Samrin regime, as demonstrated by the strong recommendation of the Parliamentary Consultative Committee on External Affairs that the government should take such a step quickly, made it easier for the Congress (I) government to implement this policy.[7]

However, ASEAN's strong and vocal opposition to the Vietnam-imposed PRK government forced India to reassess, if not to radically alter, its policy on Kampuchea. This was reflected as early as September 1980 at the Commonwealth Asian and Pacific regional meeting of heads of government (CHOGRM-II) in New Delhi. Indira Gandhi was put very much on the defensive on both the Kampuchean and Afghan issues, especially as a result of the Singapore Prime Minister Lee Kuan Yew's forthright attack on Vietnam and the Soviet Union for, what he called, 'a new doctrine of justifiable intervention outside the framework of the United Nations Charter'. Mrs Gandhi defended India's recognition of the Heng Samrin regime by arguing that, while 'she shared the concern of the ASEAN countries, upset by developments in Kampuchea', she believed that 'it would be wrong to ostracize Vietnam'. Indira Gandhi seemed to go out of her way 'to assure the conference that she was not enamoured of the Vietnamese move and had even opposed it politically'.[8] Again, at the Non-Aligned Movement (NAM) Foreign Ministers' meeting in New Delhi in February 1981, India voted with ASEAN and the majority of NAM members on resolutions calling for the withdrawal of 'foreign' troops from Kampuchea and Afghanistan, thereby indirectly endorsing criticism of the Vietnamese and Soviet military interventions in the two countries.

ASEAN's persistent opposition to the Vietnamese military presence in Kampuchea led to a realization on the part of Indian policy-makers, especially after Rajiv Gandhi's assumption of office in late 1984, that New Delhi's ostensibly undiscriminating endorsement of the Vietnamese position on Kampuchea had started to become counter-productive, especially since all it had achieved was to augment Vietnam's resolve to extend indefinitely its military presence in Kampuchea. India realized that an inflexible Vietnamese position on Kampuchea had resulted in two outcomes, both deleterious to Indian interests in the Southeast Asian region. First, it highlighted the coincidence of approaches to the Kampuchean issue between ASEAN (at least as formally represented in ASEAN's official proclamations) and China, thereby creating a potential comity of interests between non-Communist Southeast Asia and the largest Asian communist power which, in Indian perceptions, also happens to be India's principal long-term adversary.

Second, it also highlighted the convergence of Chinese and American interests in Southeast Asia because of their joint opposition to the military presence of Soviet-supported Vietnam in Kampuchea, thereby strengthening the bases for Sino-American strategic cooperation, which New Delhi viewed with considerable unease if not apprehension. Indian policy-makers, therefore, came to the conclusion that the best way of containing both the spread of Chinese influence in Southeast Asia as well as the intensification of Sino-American strategic cooperation in Asia would be to narrow the differences between Vietnam and ASEAN to such an extent as to permit the withdrawal of the bulk of Vietnamese forces from Kampuchea without compromising Hanoi's security and political interests in Indochina in general, and in Kampuchea in particular.

This Indian assessment runs almost parallel to the Indonesian assessment of the consequences of the Vietnamese invasion of, and Hanoi's continued military presence in, Kampuchea on the Southeast Asian security scene in general, and Indonesian security interests in particular. This is why from early 1987 onward India, like Indonesia and with similar objectives in mind, has also been engaged, though in a more low-key fashion, in helping to narrow the differences between ASEAN and Vietnam over Kampuchea. It sought to do this principally by acting as a conduit for the transmission of the two parties' views to each other. From the Indian perspective a compromise solution to the Kampuchean imbroglio must assuage Vietnam's security concerns, be acceptable to ASEAN and at the same time exclude, as far as possible, Chinese influence from Indochina whether through the Khmer Rouge or otherwise. With these ends in view, the Indian Minister of State for External Affairs, Natwar Singh, himself an experienced former diplomat, undertook a visit to the ASEAN capitals in March 1987.[9] This visit was preceded by a trip he made to Vietnam in January 1987 and was followed by another visit to Indochina and Thailand in July 1987.

Natwar Singh also had a meeting with Prince Sihanouk in New York on 5 October 1987 in which the latter expressed his appreciation of, and confidence in, Indian efforts to find a solution to the impasse in Kampuchea. This was the first meeting of such a high level Indian official with Sihanouk since the formation of the Coalition Government of Democratic Kampuchea (CGDK). One report emanating from New Delhi in early March 1988 and citing 'a highly placed source in the Indian external affairs ministry' stated categorically that a future round of talks between Sihanouk and PRK Prime Minister Hun Sen, who had already met twice in France, was expected to be held in New Delhi.[10] This prospect has been overtaken by events, with the informal meeting of the Kampuchean factions as well as of Vietnam, Laos, and the ASEAN countries in Bogor, Indonesia, in July 1988 and the simultaneous meeting in Jakarta of the leaders of the various Kampuchean factions with Prince Sihanouk, who had stepped down from his position as head of CGDK a few days before the Bogor meeting. However, it is interesting to note that while Sihanouk had had a meeting with the Indian Minister of State for External Affairs about two months before his first meeting with Hun Sen, the latter stopped over in New Delhi and met Indian officials on his way to Paris for the second round of his talks with the Prince.

This flurry of Indian diplomatic activity was made possible because, while on the one hand it had the confidence of Vietnam, on the other its relations with ASEAN, which had suffered as a result of the Indian recognition of the Heng Samrin regime in July 1980, improved perceptibly from 1984 onward following the appreciation on the part of both parties that differences over Kampuchea should not stand in the way of the strengthening of bilateral relations between India and the member-states of ASEAN.[11] This improvement in India–ASEAN ties was demonstrated by the visit, after a long gap, of the Thai Foreign Minister to New Delhi in May 1985 and the state visit of the Indian Prime Minister in October 1986 to Indonesia and Thailand, the first such visit to Thailand by an Indian head of government since independence. This was followed by a visit to New Delhi by the Malaysian Prime Minister in December 1986. These high-level contacts obviously paved the way for Natwar Singh's attempt to play the 'honest broker' between Vietnam and ASEAN. Furthermore, the long-standing and well-known pro-Indian sympathies of Prince Norodom Sihanouk, the President of the CGDK, provided India additional encouragement in undertaking the role of the honest broker, since New Delhi knew that it enjoyed the personal confidence of the Prince despite the latter's dependence on China and ASEAN for support.[12]

According to very high and reliable Indian sources,[13] the Vietnamese leaders gave the Indian minister the following assurances during his visit to Hanoi in January 1987 which he conveyed to the ASEAN leaders during his parleys with them in March 1987:

(a) Vietnam intended to withdraw from Kampuchea in 1990.

(b) The exclusivity of the Heng Samrin regime was no longer sacrosanct and various forms of coalitions could be discussed.

(c) Even Khmer Rouge elements, with the exception of Pol Pot, were welcome to attend discussions about the future set up in Kampuchea.

(d) Prince Norodom Sihanouk was acceptable as a negotiator about Kampuchea's future as well as a prospective partner in a Kampuchean coalition.

(e) Vietnam was interested in an early solution of the Kampuchean problem through the medium of a conference of interested parties under UN or other international auspices. Such a conference could include the five permanent members of the UN Security Council, members of ASEAN, India, Vietnam, the Phnom Penh government, various factions of the Kampuchean opposition, and 'other interested countries'.

(f) However, Vietnam made it clear that it will not withdraw from Kampuchea leaving a political and military vacuum; there must be an authority in place acceptable to Hanoi (or at least one that Hanoi can live with) before Vietnam would withdraw from Kampuchea.

(g) Vietnam would like India, among others, to be a guarantor of the Kampuchean solution, if and when one was found.

Many of these Vietnamese positions have been made public, and even modified, since they were communicated to Natwar Singh. However, the fact that they were comprehensively formulated for the first time and communicated to the Indian minister for onward transmission to ASEAN demonstrated not merely Hanoi's confidence in New Delhi but also its assessment that India carried enough credibility with ASEAN to act as a useful conduit between Hanoi and the ASEAN capitals.

The same high sources shed light on the ASEAN countries' reception of Vietnamese 'ideas' as communicated to them by the Indian minister. According to them, Indonesia and Malaysia were receptive, in varying degrees, to Vietnamese assurances. However, Singapore and Thailand were dismissive of Vietnamese ideas as 'nothing new' and, in any case, merely a 'ruse' undertaken to provide some degree of legitimacy to Hanoi's occupation of Kampuchea.

In New Delhi's perception, the range of ASEAN responses to Vietnam's 'ideas' about Kampuchea reveals an interesting pattern. Indian policy-makers attribute Thailand's negative response only partially to the fact that Kampuchea forms a buffer between Thailand and Vietnam and that, given the historical Thai suspicions of Vietnamese power, it would prefer that this neutral zone between the two countries be maintained so as to prevent Thailand from having to live in direct contact with the much superior military power of, what at least some Thais consider, an expansionist Vietnam. According to Indian officials, the Thai position is the result equally, if not more, of the military and economic benefits that Thailand reaps in its relations with the United States, by being able to portray itself as a 'frontline' state defending the frontiers of the 'free world' against a Soviet-inspired Vietnamese drive for the domination of mainland Southeast Asia. However, with increasing relaxation of tensions at the global level between the United States and the Soviet Union, this latter logic may be in danger of becoming obsolescent.

Furthermore, they believe that it provides Bangkok with the opportunity to remain on the right side of Beijing because of the demonstrated convergence of Chinese and Thai interests in regard to Vietnam and its occupation of Kampuchea. This brings dual benefits to Thailand. On the one hand, it is a demonstration, for the benefit of Washington, of Thai willingness to act as a major instrument in the implementation of the joint Sino-American strategy for the containment, and if possible roll-back, of Soviet and Soviet-allied power in the Asia–Pacific region. On the other, it acts as the best possible guarantee against the resumption of Chinese support to the Communist insurgency in Thailand, which has been plaguing the country for decades but is currently in the doldrums, at least in part because of the lack of Chinese enthusiasm for the Communist cause in a 'friendly' Thailand. In fact, the Thais have been successful, as a result of the continuing conflict in Kampuchea, in transforming the Chinese role from the principal supporter of the insurgency to a major supplier of military equipment to the Thai armed forces.[14] In Indian eyes, this seems to be, at least in part, the result of the Thai willingness to act as the conduit for the supply of Chinese arms to China's Kampuchean allies, the Khmer Rouge, who form the main force fighting the Vietnamese-supported Heng Samrin regime and the Vietnamese forces in Kampuchea.

This Indian assessment of the Thai position is based on two considerations. The first is the role that Thailand played during the Vietnam war in the 1960s and the 1970s, when it willingly allied itself with the United States and provided American forces operating against the NLF and North Vietnam with rest and recreation facilities, bases, and logistical support, in return for American military and economic aid to Bangkok. The second is the parallel that the Indians draw between the Thai support to the Kampuchean insurgency and Pakistan's support to the Afghan insurgency. According to New Delhi, the 'intransigence' demonstrated by both these countries in respect to the Kampuchean and Afghan problems respectively was aimed primarily at preventing, or at least delaying, solutions to these problems in order to demonstrate their indispensability to American global strategy. This, the Indians believe, in turn, led to massive economic and military benefits for the two countries and especially for their military-dominated regimes.

The Indians also attribute Singapore's hard-line anti-Vietnam position on Kampuchea to the Singapore leadership's 'obsessive' interest in demonstrating their country's strategic importance to the United States. According to Indian policy-makers, the highly visible and uncompromising anti-Soviet (and, therefore, anti-Vietnamese) stance adopted by Singapore is a part of this strategy. In the final analysis, the Indians argue, Singapore's position has little to do with the merits of the Kampuchean issue, but much to do with maintaining the market for Singapore goods in the West in general and in the United States in particular. This goal is of immense importance to Singapore in what is still a recessionary global situation. They feel that Singapore's leaders have come to the conclusion that the best way of maintaining, in fact enhancing, American interest in the island-republic's economic health is by playing its anti-Soviet card and by convincing the United States of the close link between Singapore's economic prosperity and its strategic value. Policy-makers in New Delhi believe, therefore, that Singapore's position on Kampuchea is basically a hostage to extraneous economic and political considerations.

In New Delhi's perception, the Philippines is too far removed and too preoccupied with other concerns to be greatly agitated by the Kampuchean problem. With mind-boggling domestic problems facing the Aquino government in its transition to democracy from the Marcos era, it has neither the time nor the inclination to involve itself in the intricate discussions surrounding the Kampuchean impasse. Moreover, the Philippine leadership is secure in the knowledge that the former American colony's strategic importance to the United States cannot be brought into question given the presence of major American naval and air bases in the Philippines. Manila will, therefore, agree to any formula adopted on Kampuchea by ASEAN whether it is conciliatory to Vietnam or antagonistic to it. Its interests in Kampuchea, in New Delhi's view, is limited to maintaining an ASEAN consensus for the sake of ASEAN unity rather than the merits of the issue itself.

Indian policy-makers are of the opinion that Brunei, ASEAN's newest member, is both new to the game of international politics and without sufficiently strong views on the Indo-Chinese situation to be directly involved in the debate on Kampuchea within ASEAN. Once again, like the Philippines, Brunei's interest in the issue is limited to its effects on ASEAN unity. It would, therefore, like Manila, contribute to any consensus on the issue that is acceptable to the other members of ASEAN.

As far as Malaysia is concerned, Natwar Singh's visit to Kuala Lumpur in March 1987 seemed to confirm the Indian assessment that differences between India and Malaysia on the Kampuchean problem were tactical rather than fundamental. More than any other ASEAN country, Malaysia had been upset by the timing of the Indian recognition of the Heng Samrin regime in July 1980. This was related to the fact that the Malaysian government had lobbied hard and successfully earlier that year to get the Indian Foreign Minister invited to participate in a dialogue with ASEAN Foreign Ministers scheduled for late June 1980 in Kuala Lumpur.[15] Consequent upon the Indian government's decision, taken some time during June 1980, to announce the recognition in early July of the Vietnamese-installed regime in Kampuchea, the then Indian Foreign Minister, Narasimha Rao, decided not to attend the meeting at Kuala Lumpur. It appears that he did so in order to avoid the dilemma of either informing the ASEAN ministers of New Delhi's impending recognition of the Heng Samrin government, thereby personally facing a barrage of criticism from the outraged gathering, or keeping mum about the issue and then being criticized equally severely for having been dishonest in his encounter with the ASEAN gathering by not communicating to them a decision already taken by New Delhi on an issue considered of such vital importance by ASEAN as a whole.

Narasimha Rao added insult to injury by making a patently flimsy excuse for his inability to attend the Kuala Lumpur meeting. The clumsy handling of the affair by New Delhi was demonstrated by the fact that the top Indian bureaucrat in charge of handling India's relations with its East Asian and Southeast Asian neighbours, who was to be Narasimha Rao's deputy in the proposed meeting with the ASEAN dignitaries and was to join the minister in Kuala Lumpur on his way back from a visit to Beijing, heard of the cancellation of Narasimha Rao's trip during a stop-over in Bangkok on his way to the Malaysian capital. He, therefore, decided to abort his own visit to Kuala Lumpur despite the Ministry of External Affairs' advice that he could continue with it if he so desired. This was truly a case, if ever there was one, of the left hand not knowing what the right hand was up to. The timing of the Indian decision to recognize PRK was particularly bad not only because it led to the India–ASEAN Foreign Ministers' dialogue being aborted but also because it came in the wake of a Vietnamese incursion into Thai territory and coincided with the visit of senior Vietnamese leaders to Moscow. This last event made it look as if the Indian recognition had been orchestrated from Moscow. New Delhi's decision, therefore, simultaneously ruffled many feathers and led to unanimous disapproval in ASEAN despite the increasingly visible differences among ASEAN capitals on the issue of dealing with Vietnam.[16]

The mishandling of this affair not merely terminated India's chances of institutionalizing a dialogue with ASEAN in the foreseeable future; it upset the Malaysians no end since they had invested so much in convincing the other members of ASEAN about the need and value of India as a dialogue partner. However, although Indo-Malaysian relations suffered for a brief spell as a result of this episode, the intensity of Malaysian reactions to having been 'let down' by India was reduced fairly quickly. While this was partially the result of the Malaysian need for the Indian market for its exports, particular palm oil, at a time when commodity prices were declining sharply, it seemed to be related as much, at least in the Indian view, to the basic convergence of Indian and Malaysian perceptions of China.

This is not a new theme in Malaysian foreign policy or in Indo-Malaysian (earlier Indo-Malayan) relations. In fact, Kuala Lumpur's apprehensions of China, initially far more acute than those of New Delhi, because of the fragile demographic balance in peninsula Malaysia and the experience of the (pre-dominantly ethnic Chinese) Communist insurgency, had been reflected earlier in Malaysia's relations with India, especially in the 1960s. The Malayan sympathy for, and support to, India during the Sino-Indian war of 1962 and the then Malaysian Prime Minister Tunku Abdul Rahman's efforts on India's behalf have been mentioned in Chapter 2. The country's politically-dominant Malay elite's fundamental and long-term negative orientation towards China has led policy-makers in New Delhi to assume that there is no basic divergence in the two country's world-views, especially as they pertain to this region. The Malaysian sponsorship of ZOPFAN (Zone of Peace, Freedom, and Neutrality) for Southeast Asia has been seen by New Delhi as a further indication of the two countries' parallel approaches to major international issues, particularly those regarding the presence of foreign powers in South and Southeast Asia.

This Indian perception was augmented by Natwar Singh's March 1987 visit to Kuala Lumpur. While the Indians perceived somewhat more unease prevalent in the Malaysian capital than they did in Jakarta regarding the continuing Vietnamese military presence in Kampuchea, they put this down to three main reasons:

(a) Malaysia being a much smaller and weaker power compared to Indonesia was likely to feel more nervous about the growth in the military capabilities and political and military influence of any regional power, whether perceived as friendly or unfriendly by Kuala Lumpur. In other words, expansion in the capabilities of any large regional power is perceived by the Malaysians as 'threatening', since intentions can change while capabilities, once acquired, tend to remain either constant or increase.

(b) Peninsula Malaysia is much nearer to Indochina and, therefore, hypothetically, much more vulnerable to presumed Vietnamese expansionism than Indonesia.

(c) Malaysia is far more sensitive than Indonesia to the feelings of its next-door neighbour, Thailand, particularly since it shares with the latter the problem of continuing Communist insurgencies and has to cooperate with Bangkok in order to combat this common problem. It cannot, therefore, afford to be seen as veering too far away from the ASEAN consensus on Kampuchea, a consensus that is primarily determined by Thailand's security needs as perceived by the Thais themselves.

Despite these differences in the Malaysian and Indonesian outlook in general, and their somewhat divergent stances on the Kampuchean issue in particular, policy-makers in New Delhi seem to be convinced that, when it comes to the crunch, the Malaysian leadership, like its Indonesian counterpart, would prefer a strong and stable Vietnam as a bulwark against Chinese expansionism into Southeast Asia to an emasculated Vietnamese entity dependent upon China's goodwill for its political and military survival.

These divergent reactions of the ASEAN countries to Natwar Singh's attempt in 1987 to act as 'honest broker' between Vietnam and ASEAN tended to reinforce New Delhi's differentiated perceptions of the various non-Communist states of Southeast Asia in terms of the congruence of the latters' interests, objectives, and orientations with those of India. While recent events, especially the Bogor meeting of July 1988, have rendered much of Natwar Singh's shuttle diplomacy redundant in terms of finding a solution to the Kampuchean impasse, the exercise and the responses it elicited from the region provided New Delhi with a good indication about which of the Southeast Asian countries were receptive to Indian diplomatic overtures and which were not. In this sense it provided a worthwhile input into the Indian foreign policy-making process.

However, the later effort launched in mid-July 1988 in New Delhi under the banner of the Non-Aligned Movement (NAM) by Zimbabwe, Cuba, and India ostensibly as a 'complementary' effort aimed at 'supporting' the Bogor meeting on Kampuchea appears to have been counter-productive as far as New Delhi was concerned and may have ended up by queering the pitch for Indian diplomacy towards ASEAN in the future. This move, which involved the current as well as the two immediately preceding chairmen of NAM, and brought together senior officials from these three countries as well as from Indonesia and Vietnam in a meeting in New Delhi, created a good deal of controversy, particularly within Indonesia. The move visibly upset some leading Indonesian figures because it was interpreted by them as an attempt to upstage Indonesia which had invested vast amounts of time and effort in getting the various parties to the Kampuchean dispute together at Bogor. The former Indonesian Foreign Minister, Mochtar Kusumaatmadja, was particularly scathing in his comments on the New Delhi meeting. He described the meeting as 'confusing and ironic' and went on to say: 'I hope they will not try to spoil what we have been doing ... in this region.'[17] The influential Indonesian language daily *Suara Pembaruan* also commented adversely on the New Delhi meeting, accusing it of 'detracting international attention from the Jakarta Informal Meeting [the Bogor meeting]'.[18] The Indonesian Foreign Minister, Ali Alatas, adopted a more diplomatic stance. He stated that the New Delhi meeting was 'a usual event' because it was a part of the non-alignment policy. He went on to say that the New Delhi meeting held on 15–16 July was complementary to the Bogor meeting which was scheduled to start on 25 July.[19]

Despite Alatas's conciliatory remarks and the participation of the Indonesian ambassador to Vietnam in the New Delhi meeting, there was public puzzlement and private resentment in Jakarta at the NAM initiative which was perceived in Indonesia, and in the rest of ASEAN, as an attempt to detract from the importance of the Bogor meeting. The Indonesian participation in the New Delhi meeting can be possibly explained with reference to Jakarta's desire not to alienate three influential members of NAM at a time when Indonesia was lobbying hard to get itself elected the next chairman of the Non-Aligned Movement in 1989.

While the Indonesians could understand the Cuban desire to derail the Bogor meeting and could forgive Zimbabwe for not being able to decipher all the intricacies of the Kampuchean issue, they were particularly upset by India's involvement in, and sponsorship of, the NAM exercise, especially since New Delhi was fully aware of the sensitivities of all sides involved in this dispute as well as a shared major objective with Indonesia *vis-à-vis* Kampuchea, namely to prevent the return of the Khmer Rouge to power following the Vietnamese withdrawal. The Indian involvement with the NAM initiative, therefore, has the potential to complicate New Delhi's relations with the ASEAN capitals, particularly Jakarta, unless India is able to convince Indonesia that it was not an attempt on the part of the NAM leaders to derail the Indonesian effort to find a solution to the Kampuchean problem.

Why India decided to participate in the NAM initiative is anybody's guess. However, one can advance a tentative explanation for the NAM meeting as well as its timing. The idea of a NAM-sponsored meeting on Kampuchea was apparently floated by its three sponsors, all of whom are on good terms with Hanoi, to provide Vietnam with an alternative venue to the Indonesian-sponsored Bogor meeting where it was felt the cards were stacked against Hanoi. It was also possibly conceived as a way of putting psychological pressure on Indonesia and the other ASEAN participants in the Bogor meeting, to force them to moderate their conditions for a Kampuchean settlement by providing Vietnam with an alternative option or instrument to pursue its objective of gradual military disengagement from Kampuchea under the right conditions. These conditions principally concern the neutralization of the Khmer Rouge as a political and military force in post-withdrawal Kampuchea.

Irrespective of whether the New Delhi meeting achieved any or all of these objectives, it appears to have been counter-productive from the point of view of Indo-ASEAN relations in general and Indo-Indonesian relations in particular. Given the importance attached to Indonesia within the overall Indian foreign policy towards Southeast Asia, it was surprising, to say the least, that New Delhi allowed itself to be mixed up with an exercise which was of only marginal significance as far as the search for a solution to the Kampuchean issue was concerned but which could have an adverse impact on India's relations with Indonesia as well as the other non-Communist countries of Southeast Asia. It seems that in this instance Indian concern for the protection of Vietnamese interests in Kampuchea outweighed the Indian desire to promote a consensus on Kampuchea between Vietnam and ASEAN by acting impartially in a dispute which is considered of vital importance to both sides.

Notes

1 For a survey of Indonesian initiatives on the Kampuchean problem and Jakarta's persistent efforts, despite misgivings in some ASEAN quarters, to maintain a dialogue with Hanoi on the issue, see Andrew J. MacIntyre, 'Interpreting Indonesian Foreign Policy: the Case of Kampuchea, 1979–1986', *Asian Survey*, vol.27, no.5, May 1987, 515–34. MacIntyre ascribes the active Indonesian diplomatic stance on Kampuchea to, what he calls, 'Sinophobia'. He argues that, 'In consequence of this outlook, the unstated resolution which Jakarta has sought for the stalemate in Indochina is one which would enable Hanoi to exercise at least de facto domination of Kampuchea. Such an outcome would serve the dual purpose of weakening the position of Beijing's protégé, the Khmer Rouge, while ensuring a robust Vietnam in a position to discourage future Chinese expansionary activities in the region' (p. 527). However, MacIntyre goes on to argue, this basic thrust of Indonesia's policy on Kampuchea is circumscribed by its equally strong commitment to the preservation of ASEAN unity (p. 530).

2 *New Straits Times*, 29 April 1986, quoted in Institute for Defence Studies and Analyses, *News Review on Southeast Asia*, May 1986, 260.

3 J. Soedjati Djiwandono, 'The Soviet Presence in the Asia–Pacific Region: an Indonesian Perspective', *Indonesian Quarterly*, vol.12, no.4, October 1984, 429, 435. In this context it is relevant to note the following remarks made by a leading Indian security analyst: 'When some of the South East Asian nations talk of the Soviet threat they often mean the Chinese threat but consider it not politic to say so in view of the current US–China state of relations. They also believe that a projection of the Soviet threat will induce a greater intimacy of security relationships with the US which will come in handy in countering the real threat which is not from the Soviet Union but from China. Very often in India in terms of popular perceptions we tend to overlook some of these diplomatic nuances and not distinguish between declaratory perceptions and real perceptions.' K. Subrahmanyam, 'Problems of International Security with Special Reference to South East Asia and South Asia', *Strategic Analysis*, vol.9, nos.2–3, May-June 1985, 122–3.

4 For details see Tridib Chakraborti, *India and Kampuchea: a Phase in their Relations, 1978–81*, Minerva Associates, Calcutta, 1985, 67–9.

5 ibid., p. 72. Also see Ramesh Thakur, 'India's Vietnam Policy, 1946–1979', *Asian Survey*, vol.19, no.10, October 1979, 969–74.

6 John W. Garver, 'Chinese–Indian Rivalry in Indochina', *Asian Survey*, vol.27, no.11, November 1987, 1207–8.

7 For a perceptive analysis of the background to the Indian decision to recognize the Heng Samrin government, see Arul B. Louis, 'Making Friends with a Neighbour's Neighbour', *Far Eastern Economic Review*, 18 July 1980, 8–10.

8 Mohan Ram, 'India Blackballed at the Club', *Far Eastern Economic Review*, 12 September 1980, 26.

9 For press reports of Natwar Singh's talks in Jakarta and Bangkok, the two ASEAN capitals considered most important for bringing about any change in the ASEAN consensus on Kampuchea, see *Straits Times*, 3 and 4 March 1987, respectively.

10 Harish Mehta, 'India Working to Help End Kampuchean Dispute', *Business Times* (Singapore), 7 March 1988.

11 This proposition was forcefully reasserted by Singapore Prime Minister, Lee Kuan Yew, during his official visit to New Delhi in March 1988. For details, see *Straits Times*, 17 March 1988.

12 An example of the confidence reposed by Prince Sihanouk in India was his reported suggestion made to Natwar Singh, Indian Minister of State for External Affairs, in early October 1987 that India, which had performed peace-keeping roles in Indochina in the 1950s and 1960s, should head an international force that would oversee the withdrawal of Vietnamese troops, prevent clashes between the Cambodian factions, ensure the country's neutrality and supervise general elections. For details, see *Straits Times*, 20 November 1987.

13 The information that follows is based on my interviews in New Delhi in May–June 1987.

14 According to the International Institute for Strategic Studies, Thailand signed an agreement with China in May 1987 for the supply of 30 T-69 tanks and 30 37mm AA guns by Beijing to Bangkok. See, *Military Balance 1987–1988*, IISS, London, p.211, Table 3. The agreement was signed during a visit to Beijing by Thailand's Army Chief, General Chaovalit Yongchaiyudh. According to a Thai scholar, 'The deal, reportedly worth 238 million baht or ... 4–5 per cent of the actual value [of armaments] came with a 10-year grace period. Thailand later purchased armoured personnel carriers [from China].' Kusuma Snitwongse, 'Thailand's Year of Stability: Illusion or Reality?' in *Southeast Asian Affairs 1988*, Institute of Southeast Asian Studies, Singapore, 1988. Another major sale of Chinese arms to Thailand was implicitly confirmed by Beijing in late April 1988. According to reports appearing in Bangkok, this deal included the supply to Thailand of 23 T-69 tanks, 360 armoured troop carriers, an anti-aircraft radar guidance system, eight mine-sweepers and 130-mm ammunition. It was also reported that the T-69 tanks would cost Thailand only US $76,000 each, about a fifth of the price of similar tanks if procured from other sources, 'China Confirms Big Arms Sale to Thais', *Straits Times*, 27 April 1988.

15 New Delhi had first sounded out ASEAN as early as 1976 about the possibility of institutionalizing a regular India–ASEAN dialogue. In March 1979, the Indian Ambassador in Jakarta submitted a memo to the ASEAN Secretariat, for the first time formally requesting that India be invited as an observer on the same basis as the United States, Japan, Australia, and the European Community to ASEAN meetings. An inaugural meeting between Indian and ASEAN officials had, in fact, taken place in Kuala Lumpur on 15–16 May 1980, approximately six weeks before the ASEAN Foreign Ministers' meeting which their Indian counterpart was expected to attend. The Indian team at this meeting was led by Eric Gonsalves, Secretary in the Ministry of

External Affairs. For details of India's political and diplomatic interaction with ASEAN during the period 1975–81, see Leo E. Rose, 'Indian and ASEAN: Much Ado About Not Much', in Robert A. Scalapino and Jusuf Wanandi, *Economic, Political, and Security Issues in Southeast Asia in the 1980s*, Research Papers and Policy Studies 7, Institute of East Asian Studies, University of California, Berkeley, 1982, 98–104.

16 For details of the ASEAN countries' reaction to the Indian recognition of PRK, see Richard Nations, 'The Price of Recognition', *Far Eastern Economic Review*, 18 July 1980, 8–9; and Tridib Chakraborti, *India and Kampuchea: a Phase in their Relations, 1978–1981*, 112–21.

17 *Jakarta Post*, 21 July 1988. In an interview he gave to Singapore's *Straits Times*, Mochtar Kusumaatmadja made the following comment on the NAM initiative: 'It is ironic that people who have never shown much interest in Kampuchea ... now that the picture is much clearer thanks to our continuing efforts, all of a sudden are taking an interest .... It puzzles me.' *Straits Times*, 19 July 1988.

18 ibid.

19 *Jakarta Post*, 15 July 1988.

7

India, the Superpowers, and Southeast Asia

Indian perceptions of Indonesian and Malaysian positions on the Kampuchean issue has led some Indian analysts and policy-makers to believe that, ironically, there may be greater commonality of interest among India, Indonesia, and Malaysia in shoring up Vietnamese resolve to stand up to China (and even to the Soviet Union, if circumstances change) than between India and the Soviet Union regarding Vietnam's future role. This Indian assessment is based upon the assumption that, in the final analysis, Moscow may not be averse to sacrificing Vietnam's interests at the altar of improved Sino-Soviet relations and the exigencies of the triangular strategic balance among the Soviet Union, the United States, and China in the Asia–Pacific theatre.

Given this clear understanding in New Delhi of the divergent objectives of the Soviet Union and India in regard to Southeast Asia in general, and Vietnam in particular, the timing of Natwar Singh's visit to ASEAN in March 1987 was surprising, since it ended up sending wrong signals to almost all ASEAN capitals. This resulted from the fact that it coincided with Soviet Foreign Minister Eduard A. Shevardnadze's visit to Indonesia and Thailand which had been advertised by Moscow as being related to the latter's search for a solution to the Kampuchean issue. The coincidence of the two visits detracted from the significance of the Indian minister's visit and conveyed the impression to members of ASEAN that both visits were planned as part of a coordinated Indo-Soviet effort to find an acceptable solution to the Kampuchean problem.

Once again, there seemed to be a foul-up at the senior political and bureaucratic levels in the Indian Ministry of

External Affairs, as a result of which all the consequences of the timing of the minister's visit failed to be analysed, and either the minister was not adequately briefed on the likely message such a visit might convey to his hosts in ASEAN or he deliberately decided to ignore the advice that he was offered. This was a serious lapse on the part of the Indian policy-makers because it tended to confuse Indian objectives regarding Kampuchea with those of the Soviets while, in reality, Indian motivations for undertaking this diplomatic foray were very different from those of the policy-makers in Moscow. The latter's primary interest in the affair lies in removing Kampuchea as a major hurdle in the process of the normalization of Sino-Soviet relations, which seems to be rather eagerly sought after by the Kremlin under Gorbachev.[1] The Indians, if anything, are worried that this Soviet quest for a rapprochement with China might prompt Moscow to put pressure on the Vietnamese to give in to major Chinese demands without an adequate *quid pro quo* ensuring the containment of Chinese influence in Indochina. This, Indian policy-makers candidly admit in private conversations, would be a disaster not only from Vietnam's point of view but that of India and the rest of Southeast Asia as well, for it could legitimize Chinese intervention in the region either directly or through its Kampuchean or other proxies.[2]

It is widely accepted in Indian policy-making circles that India has a strong interest in shoring up Vietnamese resolve not to bow to Soviet pressure to accommodate Chinese interests in Kampuchea. Unfortunately, from New Delhi's perspective, given the extent of Vietnamese economic and military dependence on the Soviet Union, the Soviet leverage with Hanoi is very substantial and can possibly be used to great effect if Moscow decides to start putting pressure on its Vietnamese ally.[3] This is one reason why India has been advising Hanoi to diversify its economic, if not military, dependence so as to reduce the Soviet leverage at least in one vital area.

Moreover, New Delhi is also aware of the immense task of reconstruction facing Vietnam which is, as one very high Indian source put to me after visiting Vietnam, 'in the stage of economic development that India had reached in 1910'.[4] The Indians are fully cognizant of the fact that rapid economic development is as essential for Vietnam to maintain its autonomy of political action as military strength, particularly when the latter is mortgaged to the goodwill of a superpower.

They also realize that the resources needed for this tremendous undertaking cannot be provided by the Soviet Union which itself faces major economic difficulties. New Delhi has, therefore, advised Hanoi that the only combination of sources that can provide it with the resources of the magnitude it needs is a US-led World Bank consortium, and that the precondition for the setting up of such a body is the normalization of Vietnam's relations with the United States. The Indian government strongly hopes that the new Vietnamese leadership would adopt a more 'rational' policy towards economic development and work towards improving its relations with Washington, so as to give it some amount of bargaining power with the Soviet Union and some capacity to resist Soviet pressures if they are brought to bear on Vietnam in the future on the issue of concessions to China.

India itself has been doing its modest share in helping to increase Vietnam's economic capabilities. From 1972 to 1987, Vietnam (earlier North Vietnam) received Indian Rs 700 million in project aid at a nominal interest rate of 5-6 per cent. Simultaneously, the Export–Import Bank of India advanced credit worth Indian Rs 450 million to Vietnam at a 9 per cent interest rate to finance project-imports from India.[5] While this may seem a drop in the ocean as far as Vietnamese needs are concerned, it is a major effort in the context of India's own requirements of capital for development projects.

The Indian ambivalence towards the Soviet Union, represented by New Delhi's advice to Vietnam, is not merely the reflection of the differences in Soviet and Indian objectives towards China; it is related as much to the Indian interest in maintaining its autonomy of action even *vis-à-vis* a friendly superpower. Augmenting Vietnam's capacity to resist Soviet pressure is in a sense a strategy to pre-empt the Soviet Union from ever applying similar pressure on New Delhi, whether in relation to China or on any other issue. This Indian attitude does not contradict its basically sympathetic understanding of the Vietnamese need for Soviet military and economic support. It is the product of the Indian interest in helping Vietnam to set certain limits on Hanoi's dependence on Moscow and to prevent the latter from taking undue advantage of the former's weakness.

In spite of these misgivings about Vietnam's excessive dependence upon the Soviet Union, Indian policy-makers generally view the Vietnamese–Soviet relationship favourably, primarily because they realize that continued Soviet military and economic support to Vietnam is essential for the latter to act as a credible bulwark against the expansion of Chinese power into Southeast Asia. This generally favourable Indian view of the Vietnamese–Soviet relationship is also the result of India's differentiated perception of the role that the two superpowers have traditionally performed in India's own regional environment and the beneficial and/or adverse effects of their respective roles on India's security and its foreign policy goals. It is also linked to the Indian sympathy for the dilemma faced by Vietnam at the end of the Second Indochina war and the close parallel, in Indian eyes, between the Vietnamese predicament and the dilemma faced by New Delhi time and again in terms of balancing India's own relationship with the Soviet Union on the one hand and with the United States and China on the other.

It is important to note in this context that the history of India's relations with the United States and the Soviet Union has led policy-makers in New Delhi to make an important distinction between the two superpowers. While extremely jealous of its autonomy and, therefore, fundamentally wary of the intentions of both the superpowers, India's experiences have led it to conclude that its aspirations regarding its self-perceived role as the preeminent power in South Asia have been constantly thwarted, intentionally or otherwise, by the United States. This was the result, first, of Washington's decision in the mid-1950s to build up Pakistan militarily, ostensibly to 'contain' the threat from the Soviet Union to the 'free world'. However, this policy resulted in the creation of a major security threat for India when Pakistan turned its American weaponry on its larger subcontinental neighbour in 1965. The Indians argue that a similar result was achieved later when the United States, according to them, 'colluded' with China during the Bangladesh crisis of 1971 to circumscribe India's capacity for autonomous action even when its vital interests were gravely threatened. To the Indians, the parallels with Vietnam's experience in this regard in the middle and late 1970s are very clear.

The Soviet Union, on the other hand, is perceived as the lesser of the two superpower evils, primarily because, in Indian perceptions, it has very rarely allowed its strategic interests in

South Asia to take priority over India's vital interests as defined by India itself. Moreover, it has been willing to concede to India the position of the preeminent power in the subcontinent and to accept, in principle, India's managerial role in the South Asian region. Furthermore, it is argued by the foreign policy-making elite in New Delhi that Moscow was ready to accept the validity of India's non-aligned policy at a time when the US still had serious reservations about it. Again, Moscow was willing to supply India with sophisticated weaponry, more or less on India's terms, to meet first the Pakistani and then the Chinese threat to its security. Therefore, according to Indian perceptions, there has been a congruence of strategic interests between Moscow and New Delhi[6] – a congruence principally achieved on India's terms – which has resulted in the preservation of India's capacity for autonomous action (although occasionally constrained as in the case of Afghanistan because of its dependence on Moscow as the principal source of arms supply) while at the same time fending off the twin Chinese and Pakistani threats to its security.[7]

As far as the dilemma faced by Vietnam after the Second Indochina War is concerned, India's policy-makers are convinced that Hanoi was forced into total dependence on the Soviet Union because of Chinese and American policies which left it with little or no option except to turn to Moscow for support. The predominant view in New Delhi is that Hanoi was reacting to Sino-American pressures when it signed a security treaty with Moscow against its original, and better, inclinations. This Indian view was expressed most strongly in a interview to the *New Straits Times* of Kuala Lumpur in May 1980 by Eric Gonsalves, then Secretary in the Indian Ministry of External Affairs, in which he 'used very strong language in criticizing China for bringing the Soviets to China's southern perimeter. The implications were that if China were to modify its stand against Vietnam, the latter would follow a more independent policy.'[8]

The Indians also strongly feel that there is a close parallel between their own experiences and those of the Vietnamese in this regard. They believe that India was also forced into signing a treaty with the Soviet Union in 1971, as a result of Sino-American collusion in support of Pakistan during the Bangladesh crisis which led to an India–Pakistan war in December that year. The draft of the treaty had been prepared by Moscow as early as 1969 but New Delhi had not shown any great enthusiasm, particularly for domestic reasons, about signing such a document until July 1971 when it became clear that war with Pakistan over the Bangladesh crisis was inevitable and that this could lead to parallel American and Chinese 'tilts' towards Pakistan.

Similarly, the Soviets had made a proposal for a friendship treaty to Hanoi in 1975 just after the fall of Saigon. The Vietnamese, like the Indians, had shelved the proposal for almost three years because they did not want to foreclose their options *vis-à-vis* China and the United States. It was only when it became clear to Vietnam that a conflict with the Pol Pot regime in Kampuchea was inevitable and that a Chinese intervention on the Khmer Rouge's behalf could not be ruled out, and also that the Americans were not averse (partially to avenge their own defeat) to China teaching Vietnam a 'lesson', that Hanoi became interested in 1978 in procuring a guarantee of support from the Soviet Union in the form of a friendship pact. To quote Nayan Chanda, 'In order to face the threat from China, Hanoi needed an insurance policy. "We took a leaf out of India's book", a Vietnamese official would later tell the Indian ambassador in Hanoi'.[9]

Given these remarkable parallels in the experiences of the two countries, it is no wonder that Indian policy-makers have such strong empathy for a Vietnam which they perceive to have been forced into Soviet arms as a result of Chinese and American policies aimed at bringing about exactly that result. This empathy is the product not so much of similar alignments with a superpower but of the similar contraction of Indian and Vietnamese options in 1971 and 1978 respectively, because of American and Chinese policies which, in Indian perceptions, forced New Delhi and Hanoi to enter into treaty relationships with Moscow which both the Asian capitals had tried hard to avoid. This is why the Indian political and bureaucratic elites feel that American and Chinese diatribes against Vietnam's treaty with the USSR and its offer of base facilities to the Soviet Union in Cam Ranh Bay and Danang are hypocritical and insincere.

In Indian perceptions there is a fundamental difference between Vietnam's lease of bases to the Soviet Union and the Philippines lease of naval and air bases to the United States. This difference lies in the fact that in the case of the latter such bases were in existence before the independence of the Philippines and, many believe, the Americans extracted an agreement from the Philippines' leaders for the continuation of these facilities as a part of the larger deal which led to the political decolonization of that country. In the case of the former, the decision was a result of Vietnam's lack of options in the late 1970s, given the combined hostility of the United States and China towards Hanoi. While India could get the best of both worlds in 1971 by persuading Moscow to sign a treaty with it without offering bases in return, Hanoi, playing an immeasurably weaker hand than New Delhi in its relations with the Soviet Union, had no option but to grant Moscow such bases as the *quid pro quo* for the treaty it so desperately needed to ward off a major Chinese threat to its security. This is why, in Indian perceptions, while the continued existence of American bases in the Philippines is deplorable because these bases do not add to, in fact may detract from, the security of the Philippines, the Soviet bases in Vietnam are acceptable as a necessary evil since they are part of a deal which provides greater security to Vietnam.

Although there is an aversion in New Delhi both to the American bases in the Philippines and to the security-links that two members of ASEAN, Thailand and the Philippines, have with Washington, of late there appears to have been considerable rethinking in New Delhi about America's overt allies in Southeast Asia. In spite of the continuing political instability in that country, the Philippines has gone up in India's esteem following the 'people power' revolution of February 1986 that brought Corazon Aquino to power in Manila. The instinctive sympathy among India's elite for democratically elected middle-class governments mouthing populist rhetoric has boosted the Philippines' image in India, although reservations continue to exist about the Aquino government's political and military linkages with the United States.

There has also been a corresponding reassessment in India regarding Thailand. This is demonstrated by the fact that, for the first time, an Indian prime minister visited Bangkok in October 1986 and that the Minister of State for External Affairs visited the Thai capital, both during his swing through ASEAN in March 1987 as well as at the end of his visit to Indochina in July 1987. In the latter instance, Thailand was the only member of ASEAN on the Indian minister's itinerary. This reassessment is, at least in part, the result of the Indian recognition that Thailand, as the ASEAN country most directly affected by the conflict in Kampuchea, is crucial to any change in the ASEAN consensus on that issue and, therefore, for the future course of ASEAN–Vietnam relations. Given India's interest in narrowing the gap between the Vietnamese and ASEAN positions on Kampuchea in order to deny China a veto on the final solution to the Kampuchean problem, New Delhi is obviously anxious to open channels of communication with Bangkok at every possible level. Therefore, one should not be surprised if in the near future Thailand becomes an important target for Indian diplomatic initiatives in the ASEAN sub-region, supplementing the primary Indian diplomatic thrust aimed at Indonesia.

Recent Indian reassessments of the international environment have not stopped with the Philippines and Thailand. Indian perceptions of the United States and, therefore, of Indo-American relations have also been subjected to a process of reassessment both by the policy-makers in New Delhi and by the larger foreign policy community in India. This reevaluation has been the result of many factors which include: (a) Indian anxieties about a likely rapprochement between the Soviet Union and China, which has encouraged Indian policy-makers to diversify their strategic and political contacts; (b) India's need for high technology which is available primarily from the West, in particular the United States; (c) the gradual liberalization of the Indian economy, which has provided a substantial boost to India's economic interactions with the West; (d) the Indian need for new markets in hard currency areas for non-traditional exports, especially manufactured products, particularly in the context of increasingly adverse balance of payments consequent upon the liberalization of the Indian economy; and (e) the easing of American restrictions on the supply of dual-use technology (that is technology that can be used for civilian as well as military purposes) to India.

This last factor has particularly acted as a major catalytic agent propelling Indo-American relations into a more positive phase. The American decision to supply such dual-use technology to India was based, in turn, on an American reassessment at the highest levels of the Reagan Administration of India's long-term value to America's global strategic interests. According to one usually well-informed observer, 'US policy makers concluded by 1984 that despite Indian unwillingness to condemn Moscow's invasion of Afghanistan, the country remained a strategic barrier to Soviet expansion to the south.... Looking to the future, US planners see India emerging as a major naval power in the region and its friendship would be valuable in maintaining US strategic interests in the Gulf and the Arabian Sea.' According to the same source, 'The result [of the American reassessment of India's value to US strategy] was a secret National Security Decision Directive No. 147 (NSDD-147) signed by Reagan on 11 October 1984. The directive instructed all US Government agencies to seek improved relations with India and accommodate Indian requests for dual-use technology. This Reagan initiative marked the beginning of a new phase in the relations [between the two countries].'[10]

The new American stance was reflected in the technological as well as the political spheres, both of which are intimately connected to the strategic dimension of the Indo-American relationship. In the technological sphere, the new stance was reflected in two major American decisions. The first was the decision taken in 1986 to grant India a licence to buy a top-of-the-line General Electric F404 jet engine for India's light-combat aircraft (LCA) currently under development. This decision was particularly significant because the US had refused to grant a licence for the same engine to China. The second decision, reportedly taken as a result of presidential intervention, was made in 1987 to sell India a Cray XMP-14 supercomputer. Although this was less powerful than the XMP-24 computer which had been India's first choice, it was the first such sale to a country outside the Western Alliance. The American policy of sale of dual-use technology to India was confirmed during the visit of US Defence Secretary Frank Carlucci to New Delhi in April 1988. During that visit Carlucci made known the US agreement to supply India with advanced ring laser gyroscopes, measuring instruments which help guide missiles and aircraft, for use in the new Indian light combat aircraft under development.[11]

In the political sphere, the new American policy was reflected in Washington's public endorsement of the India–Sri Lanka Accord which led to the deployment of Indian troops in Sri Lanka in an attempt to find a solution to the Tamil separatist insurgency. This, in effect, amounted to American's acceptance of India's role as the managerial power in South Asia,[12] even if the American definition of South Asia excluded Pakistan (which the United States tends to view more as a West Asian, rather than a South Asian, power, given Islamabad's crucial role in Washington's Gulf/West Asian strategy). On their part, the Indian policy-makers have also come to the conclusion that in view of Pakistan's importance to the United States, especially in the dual context of the conflict in the Gulf and the Soviet presence in Afghanistan, New Delhi's leverage with Washington on the issue of American military aid to Pakistan is limited. The new Indian assessment is reflected in the statement by P. K. Kaul, the Indian Ambassador to the United States, that 'Pakistan will always remain a problem [in Indo-US relations], but instead of making it the key determinant one should make it one of the 50 items'.[13] This does not mean that India will not lobby hard to limit the scope of the transfer of sophisticated American military equipment to Pakistan (as it did on the E-3A AWACS issue); it means that New Delhi will accept such arms transfers with better grace than it has done so far and will simultaneously try to obtain corresponding pay-offs (primarily in the field of dual-use technology) from the United States as well as obtain military hardware from other sources, including the Soviet Union but also Western Europe, to keep ahead – or at least abreast – of the Pakistani arsenal in both quantitative and qualitative terms.

It is felt in New Delhi that any improvement in Indo-American relations will have positive spin-offs as far as India's relations with the ASEAN countries is concerned. This is related both to the generally pro-Western foreign policy orientations of these countries as well as the congruence of their positions *vis-à-vis* Vietnam and Kampuchea with those adopted by the United States. It is related in equal measure to the fact that improving Indo-American relations help to dispel residual suspicions in non-Communist Southeast Asia about India's links with the Soviet Union, especially in terms of purchase of Soviet military equipment by New Delhi. If such links are acceptable to Washington and do not stand in the way of better Indo-American relations, the ASEAN capitals are bound to feel that they should not act as barriers to the improvement of their own political and economic relations with New Delhi.

Recent Indian attempts at playing the honest broker on Kampuchea, as well as better prospects for the solution of the

Kampuchean problem following the Sihanouk-Hun Sen meetings and the Bogor 'cocktail party', also seem to have cleared the air as far as Indo-ASEAN relations are concerned. Singapore Prime Minister Lee Kuan Yew's official visit to New Delhi in March 1988 symbolized the new assessment of India on the part of one of the most 'hard line' states in ASEAN on the Kampuchean issue. The Singapore Prime Minister made it clear to his Indian hosts that disagreement over Kampuchea between India and Singapore should not prevent good bilateral relations and increasing economic cooperation. He went on to declare: 'In any case, there will be a settlement in due course under which Vietnamese troops will withdraw from Cambodia, and we may find ourselves in agreement that Cambodia should be helped back to non-alignment.'[14] It should be noted in this context that a solution of the Kampuchean issue acceptable to ASEAN would reduce the convergence of political interests between China and non-Communist Southeast Asia, which is almost exclusively the result of the impasse on Kampuchea. This, in turn, could open up new avenues of political, and even strategic, cooperation between India and at least some of the member-states of ASEAN.

Notes

1 Improvement of Sino-Soviet relations has been a key feature of Gorbachev's strategy towards Asia, as summarized in his now-famous Vladivostok speech of 28 July 1986. For a perceptive analysis of Gorbachev's Asian strategy, see Gail W. Lapidus, 'The USSR and Asia in 1986: Gorbachev's New Initiatives', *Asian Survey*, vol.27, no.1, January 1987, 1–9, especially 2–6.

2 Such Indian misgivings also pose a problem for Gorbachev's Asian strategy, as symbolized by his Vladivostok speech. As a leading Indian journalist has argued, 'Personally, the Indian relationship represents for Gorbachev both an opportunity and a threat. If he can make gains elsewhere in Asia while preserving the relationship with India in the increasingly competitive international environment, he is likely to gain authority and prestige among his fellow Soviet leaders. Conversely, were India to respond to the threat perceived in the Vladivostok initiative by drifting away from the Soviet Union, he would likely be held responsible by his Politburo colleagues much as Nikita Khrushchev was for his Cuban missile gamble in 1962.' Dilip Mukerjee, 'Indo-Soviet Economic Ties', *Problems of Communism*, vol.36, no.1, January–February 1987, 13.

3 However, a leading American specialist on Vietnam, William Turley, is of the opinion that the Soviet–Vietnamese relationship is not as one-sided as it may appear at first sight. According to him, 'Vietnam's dependency on the Soviet Union ... is matched by the Soviet dependency on Vietnam to extend the range of its largest fleet into waters hitherto a preserve of the United States and to gain a foothold on China's southern flank. The Soviet Union has no other viable way besides cooperation with Vietnam to be a major player in this part of the world. However dependent Vietnam may be on the Soviet Union, Soviet dependency on Vietnam assures Hanoi of stable support for its own goals in Indochina.' William S. Turley, 'Vietnam/Indochina: Hanoi's Challenge to Southeast Asian Regional Order', in Young Whan Kihl and Lawrence E. Grinter, *Asian-Pacific Security: Emerging Challenges and Responses*, Archives Publishers, New Delhi, 1987, 178. It can be argued, however, that the Soviet 'dependence' on Vietnam would be radically reduced if Sino-Soviet relations improve appreciably.

4 For a bird's eye view of the problems facing the Vietnamese economy, see 'Perestroika, Doi Moi, shall we call the whole thing off?', *The Economist*, 5 March 1988, 25–6.

5 Figures provided to me by the Ministry of External Affairs, Government of India, New Delhi.

6 For an informative article on Indo-Soviet relations which argues that Gorbachev has been able to reinvigorate Moscow's close economic and political ties to India and to demonstrate the broad convergence of Indo-soviet security interests, see Jyotirmoy Banerjee, 'Moscow's Indian Alliance', *Problems of Communism*, vol.36, no. 1, January–February 1987, 1–12.

7 According to Francis Fukuyama, India's importance in Soviet foreign policy under Gorbachev has, if anything, increased. He relates this to 'Moscow's new emphasis on large, geopolitically important [Third World] states' and away from ideologically compatible states, which received major attention during the second half of the Brezhnev period. According to Fukuyama, 'The practical implications of the [new Gorbachev] policy are evident in a variety of regions around the world, nowhere more so than in India. India, of course, has been favored by the Soviets since the mid-1950s, but under Gorbachev, India has received by far the greatest amount of Soviet attention.... Gorbachev clearly views India as the centerpiece of his policy toward the developing world....Soviet leaders speaking in other Third World countries have repeatedly referred to Soviet–Indian relations as a kind of "model" for Moscow's ties with developing countries.' Francis Fukuyama, 'Patterns of Soviet Third World Policy', *Problems of Communism*, vol.36, no.5, September–October 1987, 7.

Despite the general validity of this thesis, the direct intrusion of the 'China factor' into Indo-Soviet relations, a situation not present in Soviet relations with any other Third World country except Vietnam, makes the Indo-Soviet relationship far more complicated than the way it is portrayed by Fukuyama; it also gives Indian policy-makers considerable basis for apprehension regarding a projected Sino-Soviet rapprochement – an apprehension they share with the decision-makers in Hanoi.

8 K. P. Saksena, *Cooperation in Development: Problems and Prospects for India and ASEAN,* Sage Publications, New Delhi, 1986, 62, footnote 21.

9 Nayan Chanda, *Brother Enemy: the War After the War,* Harcourt Brace Jovanovich, San Diego, 1986, 257.

10 Nayan Chanda, 'A New Indian Summer', *Far Eastern Economic Review,* 25 February 1988, 34.

11 'US Wants Military Ties with Pakistan to Go On', *Straits Times,* 9 April 1988.

12 This is a policy that has been advocated by a number of American specialists on South Asia. According to one, 'Above all, Washington needs an India policy that will facilitate New Delhi's difficult role of building a regional consensus on security issues in Asia – including a response to the Soviet presence in Afghanistan.... A US policy recognising India's position as the natural arbiter of political conflicts in the area can create more room for problem-solving through negotiation, India's preferred style, and provides the best hope for stability in a potentially explosive environment. A new India policy comparable to the bold China opening of the 1970s could highlight common interests that are almost entirely obscured by the trilateral Pakistan–India–US framework. At stake is America's interest in the emergence of a strong, stable, democratic, and non-aligned India, an interest that America, until now, was able to relegate to the distant "long term". That long term is upon us.' Francine R. Frankel, 'Play the India Card', *Foreign Policy,* no.62, Spring 1986, 166.

13 Quoted in Nayan Chanda, 'A New Indian Summer', *Far Eastern Economic Review,* 25 February 1988, 35.

14 *Straits Times,* 17 March 1988.

8

India and Southeast Asia: Concluding Remarks

India's economic relations with Southeast Asia, particularly with the ASEAN countries, have also provided an input, although a secondary one, into the formulations of Indian policy-makers perceptions of Southeast Asia (see Chapter 2). This is the result of the continued growth of India's economic transactions with ASEAN from the mid-1970s onward. By 1982 the ASEAN countries' share of India's exports, which had been 2.6 per cent in 1970, had risen to 4.2 per cent. During the same period, their share of India's total imports had risen even more dramatically, from 0.6 per cent to 5.9 per cent.[1] According to the figures computed by the Government of India's Ministry of Commerce, India's exports to ASEAN countries in the Indian financial year 1985–6 accounted for 2.9 per cent of its total exports. India's imports from ASEAN during the same period constituted 4.6 per cent of its total imports. The balance of trade, which had shifted against India in the second half of the 1970s, has continued with India importing about three times as much from ASEAN as a whole as it exported in 1985–6.[2] However, the growth in bilateral trade, especially in terms of absolute value, while highlighting its mutually beneficial character, does not put ASEAN, or the whole of Southeast Asia for that matter, in the category of an indispensable trading partner as far as India is concerned.

Indian joint ventures, particularly with Malaysia and Indonesia and now increasingly with Thailand, give added content to Indo-ASEAN economic transactions. Southeast Asia has seen the largest concentration of Indian joint ventures, based on transfer of appropriate technology and skills from

India to countries of this region. Once again, while important in their own right, these ventures are but marginal to the overall performance of the Indian economy and their absence would hardly be noticed in India, except by the corporations directly concerned, if they disappeared overnight.

Moreover, the limitations on India's capacity for such joint ventures is clearly recognized in New Delhi, particularly in the context of competition faced by India from Japan in this regard. India cannot compete successfully with Japan or with the other industrialized countries in terms of export of either capital or high technology, dependent as it is itself on the import of these two critical commodities. All it can do is to capitalize on the fact that it can provide both relevant technology and skills cheaper than the industrialized countries, a consideration that has become increasingly important to the recession-hit economies of ASEAN during the last few years. But, once again, New Delhi's capacity to acquire leverage with Southeast Asian countries based on such ventures is extremely limited and is recognized in India as being so.

Therefore, New Delhi has come to the conclusion that if it is to have some clout in Southeast Asia and carry some weight in terms of the foreign policy calculations of Southeast Asian states, it would have to demonstrate its relevance to the region in political, rather than economic, terms. It is this conclusion that broadly informs Indian policy towards the region today. It is only when one recognizes the primacy of the political in India's approach towards Southeast Asia, indeed towards the Asia–Pacific region as a whole, that all the pieces constituting Indian policy towards both Southeast Asia and the Asia–Pacific region fall into place and one is able to construct a relatively clear picture of what India's major objectives are in relation to this region, whether they are related to Southeast Asia *per se* or are derivative of larger Indian political and security interests. Such an understanding also provides the most important clues about the way New Delhi has gone about operationalizing its foreign policy strategy *vis-à-vis* Southeast Asia.

Viewed in this light, it becomes clear that Indian interest in Southeast Asia is expected to increase in the coming decade primarily for political and strategic reasons, especially if the Chinese capacity for influence in this region expands following even a partial success of its 'four modernizations' programme[3] and even a limited rapprochement in Beijing's relations with

Moscow. Furthermore, New Delhi does not view Southeast Asia any longer as a self-contained foreign policy arena towards which it can shape its policy independently of its wider strategic concerns regarding the larger Asia–Pacific region – of which Southeast Asia, in Indian perceptions, forms an integral part. Therefore, India's involvement with Southeast Asia is bound to grow, given the greater importance in strategic terms that the Asia–Pacific region has acquired in the last decade – a trend that is likely to continue and accelerate during the next decade. The growing strategic importance of the Asia–Pacific region is related to the phenomenal economic performance of the region in the past two decades, its tremendous economic potential as well as its geography, which encompasses the Soviet Far East as well as the American West Coast plus the third global nuclear power, China, and the most dynamic economic and technological power in the world, Japan. In addition to all this, a much greater amount of superpower attention is likely to be lavished on Asia–Pacific, following the expected reduction in tensions in Europe consequent upon superpower agreement, in the form of the INF Treaty, on the elimination of medium and short-range nuclear missiles as well as the increasing momentum of superpower negotiations regarding the reduction, if not elimination, of strategic weaponry.

With a superpower detente on the cards in Europe, the Asia–Pacific region, including Southeast Asia and spilling over into the Indian Ocean and the countries surrounding it, has within it all the ingredients that could make it the epicentre of the next phase of great power competition for influence and power within the international system. The situation is likely to be more complicated in this region than in Europe because of the presence of at least two additional actors, China and Japan, capable, actually or potentially, of pursuing their own objectives relatively free from effective superpower control and possessing the capacity to influence events beyond their immediate neighbourhood. With one of these actors, China, perceived by India as basically hostile in the long-term, and the other, Japan, still an unknown quantity in terms of its strategic orientation over the long haul,[4] New Delhi's concern about the effects of this quadrilateral power game in the Asia–Pacific region on India's vital interests is expected to be qualitatively different from its interest in the earlier phases of global superpower rivalry centred on far-away Europe.

It is worthwhile to note in this context that some observers in New Delhi believe that a strong, nuclear capable and strategically autonomous Japan would be in India's long-term interest, especially because it would divert Chinese attention and energies away from South and Southeast Asia towards Japan. This conclusion is based on the assumption that, while Beijing would like to see Japan possess sufficient power to contribute to the neutralization of Soviet capabilities in Northeast Asia, it would like Japanese capabilities to supplement and not substitute for, far less supplant, American capabilities in the Asia–Pacific region. China would also like the United States to keep tight control over growing Japanese defence capabilities, so that they do not begin to take on a life of their own independently of the larger Western security concerns in the Asia–Pacific region.[5] This, however, could prove a difficult condition to sustain, especially if, within the concept of 'burden sharing' with the United States, the growth of Japanese power crosses that invisible line where it begins to gain a momentum of its own, even if initially it continues to conform to the overall American strategic design. Such an eventuality could not only alienate China, it could also force the United States to choose between China and Japan if Sino-Japanese relations deteriorate. Since on present calculations, based on a comparative estimate of the two countries' currently mobilizable capabilities, Tokyo is of far greater strategic importance to Washington than Beijing, the United States could be logically expected to choose Japan over China if such a choice is forced upon it.[6] Therefore, any deterioration in Sino-Japanese relations, some Indians argue, could dramatically weaken China's leverage with Washington and work to India's advantage in the long term.

Furthermore, India does not consider itself to be in competition with Japan in Asia which, to quote a senior Indian bureaucrat, is 'in a different league altogether',[7] a description which, in Indian perceptions, does not apply to China. Moreover, there are no legacies of Japanese imperialism or occupation in India, as is the case with Southeast Asia,[8] which could cloud Indian perceptions of Japan. It is important to note that the Indian judge on the Tokyo War Crimes Tribunal, Justice Radhabinod Pal, gave a sharply dissenting judgement from the majority of the Tribunal on the issue of Japanese war crimes. He held that the Japanese leaders were not guilty of war crimes and that the decision to hold them so was an act of political retribution that would not stand the test of international law.[9] Although India did not sign the 1951 San Francisco Peace Treaty with Japan, holding it to be a Cold War device, it signed a bilateral treaty in June 1952 terminating the state of war with Japan and renouncing all Indian claims for war reparations.

While Indian perceptions of Japan during the 1960s and 1970s were coloured by Tokyo's strategic alignment with Washington, Japan's acquisition in the 1980s of massive economic and technological clout and the more perceptible flexing of its political and military muscle has begun to convince a significant segment of the Indian foreign policy community that Japan is bound to play an independent role in the foreseeable future in the Asia–Pacific strategic-political arena.[10] Some Indian strategic analysts go on to argue from this premise that Japan can be turned into a significant economic and political asset for India and that, therefore, there is a strong need to build closer ties to Tokyo. This reevaluation of Japan's image by New Delhi was aided by the visit of the former high-profile Japanese Prime Minister, Yasuhiro Nakasone, to India in May 1984, the first visit by a Japanese head of government to India in twenty-three years, and Indian Prime Minister Rajiv Gandhi's return visit to Japan in November 1985. Since then Rajiv Gandhi has visited Japan twice again, the last time in April 1988 to inaugurate a 'Festival of India' in Tokyo. The fact that Japan accounted for about 8 per cent of India's total trade in the first half of the 1980s has augmented Indian interest in that country,[11] although Japan's trade with, and investment in, South Asia in general, and India in particular, 'has failed to match either the growth in its aid budget or the overall potential'.[12]

The growing importance of Japan in the eyes of top Indian policy-makers is borne out by the fact that in 1987 the ultimate responsibility in the Indian Ministry of External Affairs for overseeing matters relating to Japan was transferred from Secretary (East), in whom it had been traditionally vested, to the Foreign Secretary, the Ministry's top bureaucrat who, incidentally, had just completed two consecutive tours of duty as ambassador to Japan and China. What was more important was that this was done at the behest of Prime Minister Rajiv Gandhi himself at the time of K. P. S. Menon's appointment as the new Foreign Secretary.

It is also realized in New Delhi that no matter which way Japan moves strategically in the 1990s, the effects on the Indian subcontinent of the evolving quadripartite power game in the Asia–Pacific region are likely to be geographically mediated through Southeast Asia. New Delhi has, therefore, evinced a strong desire to bolster the capacity of the larger Southeast Asian countries, principally Indonesia and Vietnam, as far as possible to insulate themselves and, therefore, their region from the unwelcome effects of the projected big power rivalry. India perceives itself as sharing with these countries the goal of maintaining, in as great a measure as possible, their capacity for autonomous action *vis-à-vis* the dominant global and Asia–Pacific powers. Their shared antipathy towards China in particular augments the Indian view that the three countries' perceptions of the Asia–Pacific region and their place in it are broadly similar if not totally identical. As a result, one can safely project that Indonesia and Vietnam, irrespective of the nature of their regimes, would continue to be the central foci of Indian policy towards Southeast Asia for some time to come.

This does not mean that Indian policy-makers are not aware of potential points of friction and/or rivalry with the major Southeast Asian powers, especially Indonesia whose security perceptions have at times sharply diverged from those of India, as was the case in last years of the Sukarno era. They also know that segments of the Indonesian military leadership still periodically demonstrate a sense of unease and suspicion about growing Indian power projection capabilities. Despite these problems which are anticipated by New Delhi, the general feeling among the Indian foreign policy community seems to be that any friction or rivalry between India and Indonesia in the future will be kept within limits, because of the realization in both Jakarta and New Delhi that there is a basic convergence of Indian and Indonesian interests over fundamental issues of foreign policy, especially as they pertain to the larger Asia–Pacific region and the quadrilateral power play within this extended regional theatre.

However, there are several factors, many of which have been mentioned earlier, operating within Southeast Asia and outside – factors over which New Delhi has little or no control – that are full of uncertainties and that can affect India's relations with individual countries of Southeast Asia as well as with the region as a whole. The foremost among these include the future course of the dispute over Kampuchea, the evolution of Sino-Soviet relations and of Chinese policy towards Southeast Asia, the strategic future of Japan and last, but not the least, domestic political and economic developments within the countries of Southeast Asia.

If the current positive trend, from the Indian perspective, of dialogue among the various Kampuchean factions, especially between Prince Sihanouk and the Phnom Penh regime, as well as the convergence of Vietnamese and Indonesian interests regarding a solution of the Kampuchean problem persists, it might provide India with a more favourable environment within which to conduct its diplomacy in Southeast Asia. This would be so only if New Delhi does not queer the pitch for itself by indulging in basically futile exercises like the trilateral NAM initiative of July 1988. This positive trend will be substantially strengthened if the Vietnamese withdraw the bulk of their troops from Kampuchea in 1990, as they have repeatedly declared is their intention to Indian and other visiting dignitaries. However, if, on the other hand, this trend is reversed and if a consensus among various parties to the Kampuchean dispute fails to materialize within a reasonable period of time and, therefore, if Hanoi goes back on its commitment to withdraw its troops by 1990, ASEAN and Vietnamese positions on Kampuchea are bound to harden. If the latter scenario is played out in Indochina, it could considerably curtail the Indian capacity for diplomatic maneouvering in Southeast Asia, especially since the Indonesians (who share India's empathy for Vietnam) would also be put off if their Bogor initiative fails as a result of the inflexibility of the Vietnamese position on the Kampuchean issue.

Similarly, as long as China remains embroiled in its own domestic economic and political contradictions, and its relationship with the Soviet Union and Vietnam continues to remain cool if not hostile, the Indian policy-makers can afford to take a relaxed view of the Chinese capacity to influence events in Southeast Asia. However, if these domestic and external constraints on Chinese foreign policy capabilities are reduced, if not totally removed, Beijing, according to Indian perceptions, can be expected to become increasingly assertive in its neighbourhood and to throw its weight around in Southeast Asia at the expense of other extra-regional actors, including India. This would particularly be the case if China's modernizations policy succeeds even partially for, as Jonathan Pollack has pointed out, 'The Chinese leadership has determined that China's emergence as an independent major power represents the most important policy consideration for the remainder of the twentieth century, to which all other objectives must be subordinated.'[13]

Japan's capacity to influence the economic and regional security environments of Southeast Asia has been discussed earlier. While India would generally welcome an autonomous Japanese political and strategic role in the region,[14] it is by no means certain that Japan's high economic and technological profile would be automatically followed by an independent political and strategic stance. Tokyo might decide that it is in Japan's interest to continue to follow the American lead as far as political–security issues are concerned, both because it is strategically vulnerable and because it does not want to augment the existing negative dimensions of its image in America, which are the result primarily of its economic performance and its huge trade surplus with the United States.

Furthermore, there is no guarantee that a politically and strategically autonomous Japan may not decide that it is in its interest to cooperate with, rather than confront, China.[15] Tokyo might come to this conclusion in order to set limits to the influence of both the superpowers in the Asia–Pacific region or, as is even more likely, to balance Japan's basically hostile relationship with the Soviet Union. Tokyo's relations with Moscow have been profoundly affected by Soviet–Japanese differences regarding the future of the four northern islands captured by the Soviet Union from Japan during the closing days of the Second World War. Soviet and Japanese positions on the disputed islands have remained inflexible for the last four decades and show little sign of undergoing any major transformation in the foreseeable future. Therefore, despite the general East–West thaw since Gorbachev's assumption of office as well as the long- standing Soviet interest in acquiring Japanese high technology and the Japanese desire for greater access to the potentially vast Soviet market, the stalemate on this issue continues to bedevil Soviet–Japanese relations.[16]

China's importance in the overall Japanese economic and political strategy had been demonstrated earlier when Tokyo established diplomatic relations with Beijing in September 1972 close on the heels of American President Nixon's visit to China and several years before the establishment of formal diplomatic ties between the United States and China. It also signed a Peace and Friendship Treaty with Beijing in August 1978 to the considerable chagrin of Moscow, especially since the treaty, as a result of Chinese insistence, contained an 'anti-hegemony' clause (Article 2), which was interpreted as a thinly veiled attack on the Soviet Union.[17] The development of Sino-Japanese political, economic and technological relations in the second half of the 1970s and the first half of the 1980s has, in fact, led a German specialist on Japan to conclude that, 'The Japanese–China relationship represents the closest so far between a major Communist and a major capitalist country.'[18] A leading Japanese specialist on security affairs has underscored this point by stating that, 'Tokyo regards Deng Xiaoping's pragmatic leadership as important for Japan's security, and believes that his efforts at building a stable and viable economy will also stabilize Chinese politics. A predictable China, friendly to Japan, serves as a significant shield against the Soviet Union.'[19]

If Japan continues to stress the importance of China in its economic and political strategy, it could upset the nascent calculations made by some members of the foreign policy community in India about Japan's future role as the main constraint on Chinese capabilities in the Asia–Pacific region. It may, in fact, force New Delhi to face up to the prospect of a potentially hostile regional coalition in Asia. This, in turn, could increase India's strategic dependence on the Soviet Union, thereby curtailing its diplomatic and political flexibility. Moreover, with increasing Soviet interest in normalizing relations with China, the degree of Soviet support to India in the face of a hypothetical Sino-Japanese axis may not be enough to offset the negative impact of such a coalition on India's security concerns.

As far as the domestic scenes in the various Southeast Asian countries are concerned, Indian policy-makers, like most others around the world, tend to take them, with the possible exception of the Philippines and Kampuchea, as by and large constant. Consequently, they also take as given the division of the region between Communist Indochina and non-Communist ASEAN, with Burma playing a peripheral political role while indulging in its increasingly costly ideological eccentricities. Although this may be a correct prognosis, changes within Southeast Asian countries cannot be totally ruled out. Such changes, and especially their effects on the international orientations of the affected countries, cannot be wholly foreseen by Indian, or for that matter other external, policy-makers. If major transformations occur in one or more Southeast Asian countries, the basic assumptions of Indian policy towards that particular country, or even the entire region, may have to be reassessed.

Furthermore, like all policy-makers, Indian decision-makers face the problem that their perceptions may not be fully congruent with Southeast Asian realities or that their perceptions of the Southeast Asian elites' perceptions regarding important regional and global issues may not coincide with the reality of the latters' perceptions. In such cases, especially when they relate to important Southeast Asian actors like Indonesia and Vietnam, the assumptions on which Indian policies towards them (or towards major regional issues like Kampuchea in which they are involved) are based may, hypothetically, turn out to be so erroneous as to do grave damage in the long run to India's relations with these specific countries or with the region as a whole. These are dangers of which one would assume the policy-makers in New Delhi are aware, even if they do not always give adequate indication of such awareness. Again, given the relative openness of the Indian decision-making apparatus to differing views both within and outside the government, there is a certain amount of flexibility built into the policy-making system at the tactical level that could possibly minimize the deleterious effects of such perceptual incongruence and prevent major damage to India's relations with the more important Southeast Asian states.

These caveats have been raised in the last few paragraphs to demonstrate not so much that Indian policy-makers are unaware of these variables, which might make a difference to the success or otherwise of Indian policy towards Southeast Asia, but to highlight two things: one, that much of Indian policy towards Southeast Asia is derivative of other interests and objectives that New Delhi considers of higher priority in terms of its foreign policy calculations. Two, that even where Indian policy is largely determined by factors internal to Southeast Asia, it is of necessity hostage to these factors, which are largely beyond India's control and are themselves influenced by a large number of other variables, many extra-regional in character. Therefore, no intelligent analysis can afford to treat Indian policy towards Southeast Asia in isolation from the broader framework of Indian foreign policy and the larger calculus of Indian strategic interests, as well as from the overall international and regional contexts in which Indian foreign policy is made and implemented. If this larger picture of interests and calculations and the global and/or regional contexts of policy change over time so would India's perception of Southeast Asia's importance to it and this, in turn, would affect, for better or for worse, the broad contours of Indian policy towards this region.

Despite the dependence of India's Southeast Asian policy on the larger issues that affect India's overall foreign policy and strategic framework, Southeast Asia does have major relevance for India's national interests – despite the fact that India's policy-makers did not pay adequate attention to this region in the 1960 and 1970s. But, as this book has argued, there have been important changes in Indian perceptions regarding Southeast Asia during the last decade that have elevated the relative importance of this region in Indian strategic and foreign policy calculations. While India's renewed concern about China, in the wake of the latter's modernizations policy and the thaw in Beijing's relations with Moscow, have contributed substantially to New Delhi's reassessment of the importance of Southeast Asia to Indian interests, this is not the only reason for such reevaluation. The expansion of India's military, technological, and economic capabilities as well as the end of the oil bonanza in the Gulf have also been responsible for India's growing interest in the Asia–Pacific area in general, and Southeast Asia in particular. The impressive economic growth of the Asia–Pacific region and the emergence of Japan as an economic and technological superpower (and a potential major political and strategic actor at regional and global levels) have also forced India's policy-makers to sit up and take notice not merely of East Asia but of Southeast Asia as well, especially since the latter forms both an integral part of the Asia–Pacific and the geographic and cultural bridge between India and the wider Pacific community.

The political and economic future of Southeast Asia is, therefore, viewed by New Delhi as closely linked to India's own future, especially in terms of India's prospective strategy aimed at coming to grips with the emerging multipolar power equation centred in the Asia–Pacific region. This perception will be augmented if India's policy-makers come to the conclusion at the turn of the decade that the formulation of such a strategy is the most important challenge that they would have to face in the 1990s and that India's standing in the international hierarchy of power will depend crucially on the success or failure of New Delhi's Asia–Pacific strategy.

Notes

1 Charan D. Wadhva, 'India's Trade with South and Southeast Asia', in Malcolm Adiseshiah (ed.) *Role of Foreign Trade in the Indian Economy*, Lancer International, New Delhi, 1986, 64.

2 Government of India, Ministry of Commerce, *Annual Report 1986–7*, 91–2 and 97–9.

3 For an optimistic view of the likely success of China's modernization programme, see Albert Keidel, 'China's Economy in the Year 2000', in David M. Lampton and Caterine H. Keyser (eds), *China's Global Presence: Economics, Politics, and Security*, American Enterprise Institute For Public Policy Research, Washington DC, 1988, 67–79. For a more guarded assessment, which takes into account the political uncertainties plaguing post-Mao China, see David M. Lampton, 'Driving Beyond the Headlights: the Politics of Reform in China', in the same volume, For Lampton, Deng Xiaoping's statement in a conversation with George Shultz on 3 March 1987 best sums up the current situation in China. The Chinese leader told the American Secretary of State: 'As far as the troubles here, they are almost finished, *but maybe it will take years.* They existed for a long time,' 21, (italics added).

4 A keen observer of the Japanese scene has summed up the domestic climate of opinion in Japan regarding its future strategic posture in the following words: 'Politically, a sort of consensus has slowly emerged that the country's security is best guaranteed by remaining a junior partner of the US. But the Left has continued to advocate neutrality and recently some among the Right and centre have been tempted to opt for autonomous defence. Disputes with the US over burden-sharing, feelings of nationalism which these disputes heightened, and fear of increased vulnerability to Soviet nuclear attack ... have all contributed to the new urge to go it alone. East–West detente may also encourage autonomous defence.' Susumu Awanohara, 'The Dangers of a Frustrated Tokyo', *Far Eastern Economic Review*, 30 April 1987, 76.

5 As R. Taylor has argued, 'The defence of Japan itself, especially in the face of the increased Soviet power, is acceptable to the Chinese; but a greater independent Japanese military role in the region would

be viewed with suspicion.' R. Taylor, *The Sino-Japanese Axis: a New Force in Asia?*, St Martin's Press, New York, 1985, 100.

6 For details of this argument, see my comments on William Tow's chapter in David M. Lampton and Caterine H. Keyser (eds), op. cit., 191–3.

7 In private conversation with the author, June 1987.

8 For a recent illustration of residual Southeast Asian suspicions regarding the renewed growth of Japanese power, see Seah Chiang Nee, 'Mighty Japan is Both Partner and Threat to Asia', *International Herald Tribune*, 23 March 1988.

9 For details of Justice Pal's judgement, see *The Tokyo Judgement: the International Military Tribunal for the Far East, 29 April 1946–12 November 1948, Vol.2*,, APA–University Press Amsterdam BV, Amsterdam, 1977, 517–1039.

10 For example, a leading Indian analyst of strategic affairs, while delivering the keynote address at the silver jubilee symposium of the National Defence College in New Delhi in April 1985, made the following remarks: 'At this stage, it is still not received wisdom to talk of the conflict between the US and Japan assuming dimensions when Japan will start asserting an independent role in the global strategic balance and attempt to manoeuvre among the US, China, and USSR in such a way as to enlarge its commercial and technological advantages. It is, however, difficult to see how that development can be avoided.... The future course of US–Japanese trade and technological rivalry will be the basic factor determining the security environment of South East Asia.... If Japan is forced to retrench its trade with the US and Western Europe and observe restraints, it is bound to turn its attention increasingly to areas where it will have an opportunity to continue to expand. This will mean primarily China, South East Asia and even the Soviet Union.... It is unrealistic to assume that US–Japanese trade and technological rivalry can be managed without tension and international realignments, though perhaps in the nuclear age one can rule out war among the industrialised nations.' K. Subrahmanyam, 'Problems of International Security with Special Reference to South East Asia and South Asia', *Strategic Analysis*, vol.9, nos 2–3, May–June 1985, 123–4, 129, 130.

11 Savitri Vishwanathan, 'Continuity and Change: India's Relations with Japan', *India Quarterly*, vol.41, no.1, January–March 1985, 26.

12 Nigel Holloway, 'Seeking Friends and Influence: Japan Takes a More Active Interest in Southwest Asia', *Far Eastern Economic Review*, 12 May 1988, 26. According to Holloway, 'The brightest development [in India–Japan relations] has been the rapid growth in Japan's official development assistance to the [South Asian] region, from US$ 410 million in 1983 to US$ 831 million in 1986, and it is the leading donor there. Aid to India alone this year [1988] is expected total around Y100 billion (US$ 802 million).'

13 Jonathan D. Pollack, 'China's Changing Perceptions of East Asian Security and Development', in Douglas T. Stuart, *Security within the Pacific Rim*, Gower, Aldershot, 1987, 54–5.

14 A leading Indian scholar of Japan has argued in this context that, 'Although Japan is a member of the Western bloc of nations, it is not a western nation. Japan has to be cultivated as Japan and not as a Western appendage. Japan's thought patterns, responses, etc., are based on its own culture. A more successful [Indian] inter-action with Japan can be achieved if this aspect is given careful consideration. Frustrations and disappointments would arise if Japan is expected to react and respond like a nation of the West.' Savitri Vishwanathan, op. cit., 26.

15 That Sino-Japanese cooperation, particularly in the economic sphere, is mutually beneficial is borne out by the fact that, 'By the early 1980s a third of Chinese imports came from Japan, which in turn was taking 20 per cent of China's exports; even more importantly Sino-Japanese trade accounted for over half of China's total trade with Western industrial countries.' R. Taylor, op. cit., 102.

Furthermore, according to the latest statistics available, in 1986 Japan's trade with China amounted to four and one-half times its trade with India. During that year Japan's exports to China were worth 1,667 billion yen and its imports from China totalled 966 billion yen, making a grand total of 2,633 billion yen. The corresponding figures for India were 353 billion yen and 223 billion yen, which meant that the total value of Japan's trade with India amounted to only 576 billion yen. These figures have been taken from *Japan Statistical Yearbook 1987*, Table 10-3, 336-7.

16 For a perceptive analysis of Japan's problems with the Soviet Union and their likely effects on Japan's future strategic posture, see Robert O'Neill, 'Japan Peeps Over its Horizon', *International Herald Tribune*, 28-9 May 1988. O'Neill comes to the conclusion that the legal and constitutional obstacles to Japan's rearmament 'could be overcome by political action without great impact on Japanese politics if the [Japanese] public continues to view the Soviet Union as a potential enemy and is worried that the United States will leave Japan increasingly to fend for itself'.

17 As a *quid pro quo* the Japanese demanded the inclusion of Article 4, which stated that, 'The present treaty shall not affect the position of either contracting party regarding its relations with third countries.' This, however, was not enough to assuage Moscow's anger and the latter not only threatened 'retaliatory action' against Japan, it noted that, 'The future will show whether Japan will be able to pursue an independent foreign policy'. See, Chalmers Johnson, 'Japanese–Chinese Relations, 1952–82', in Herbert J. Ellison, *Japan and the Pacific Quadrille*, Westview Press, Boulder, Colorado, 1987, 120.

18 Reinhard Drifte, 'Japan's Relations with the East Asia–Pacific Region', in Douglas T. Stuart, op. cit., 28.

19 Masashi Nishihara, 'Prospects for Japan's Defence Strength and International Security Role', in Douglas T. Stuart, op. cit., 44.

Index

All references are to India unless otherwise stated

and Kampuchea 53–4, 57, 67, 68,
    70n: assurances 59–61, 91;
    invasion of 36, 55
and Malaysia 65–6
nationalism 38, 50n
navy 49n
perceived role 35, 36, 38
relations with China 32
relations with India 23, 39, 53, 90
relations with US 74, 77
and Soviet Union: dependence on
    74, 76, 77–8, 83n; support 58,
    73, 74, 75, 76
war 39, 62

Vishwanathan, Savitri 98n

West Bengal 5
West/Western 4, 5
    alliances 10
    presence in Asia 2
World Bank consortium 74

Yongchaiyudh, Chaovalit 70n
Younger, George 46

Zimbabwe 66, 67
ZOPFAN (Zone of Peace Freedom
    and Neutrality) 12, 65